GESTAPO

THE HISTORY OF THE GERMAN SECRET SERVICE

GESTAPO

THE HISTORY OF THE GERMAN SECRET SERVICE

Philip St. C. Walton-Kerr

BRACKEN BOOKS
LONDON

Gestapo

First published in 1939 by Robert Hale Ltd, London

This edition published in 1996 by Bracken Books, an imprint of
Random House UK Ltd, Random House,
20 Vauxhall Bridge Road, London SW1V 2SA

Copyright © Philip St. C. Walton-Kerr 1939

ISBN 1 85170 545 7

Printed and bound in Guernsey by The Guernsey Press Co. Ltd

CONTENTS

7

CONTENTS

AUTHOR'S FOREWORD

A COMPLETE history of German espionage would demand not merely a book, but a whole library. This survey can do no more than outline the outstanding facts and figures of that evil system: "evil," not only because of its methods, which involve a definite retrogression from the point to which Latin civilization has reached, but also because of the ends to which it has been consistently directed since Stieber began his work for the Iron Chancellor, before the term "German Emperor" was coined.

In such a brief survey, it is possible to confine the work and the methods of Stieber and his successors to study of the spy system and nothing else, only up to the end of the last war, 1918. Until then, the spy system, although a very important part of the national life of Germany, was a separate part of that life, and thus can be considered separately. It has been so considered, and in Part I of this work has been condensed as much as possible, with regard for the far greater interest attaching to Nazi and Gestapo activities (entirely separate as these two are) since, say, 1930. With the growth of the National Socialist Party, which dominates Germany of today, there grew up a new organization, the GEheim STAats POlizei, or GE-STA-PO, so intricately bound up with and part of the whole political system that independent study of it, as distinct

9

from German world policy, is an impossibility. To realize to the full its aims and accomplishments, one must realize those of the German leaders of to-day.

As instance: it is necessary, for comprehension of the power and purposes of the Gestapo, to state the causes leading up to the "June Purge" of 1934, and to detail the aims of those responsible for this bloody business— and, it is the author's belief, for the first time to reveal the facts of that night, facts utterly at variance with the account issued by Goebbels in his capacity of propagandist for the Third Reich. Goebbels, by the way, had better luck over his version of the June Purge than with his account of the burning of the Reichstag: he managed to get the former believed, both in his own country and outside it; nobody, even in Germany, could stomach the account of the latter happening.

The first part of this book, an account of the German spy system originated by Karl Stieber and maintained up to the downfall of the Imperial régime in 1918, is a very brief summary of facts drawn from various sources. Among these may be mentioned Stieber's *Memoirs*, translated into French, but not, as nearly as can be ascertained, into English; *Indiscretions* by Wollheim, which throws a little light on the system; Paul Lanoir's *German Spy System in France*, which is a very good summary indeed of the work indicated by the title; Klembovski's *Military Espionage in Peace and War*, which outlines the duties connected with military espionage, and illustrates the doctrine by incidents, sometimes highly illuminating; a very lucid summary of German activities from Stieber's origin to about 1914, entitled *The German Spy System from Within*, anonymous as regards the author, and published by Hodder & Stoughton early in 1915 (apparently) but now, unfortunately, out of print; newspaper reports of the period 1914-18 have furnished some very useful material, and a Home Office statement of the formation and objects of our own Special Branch, issued in 1914, have all been used by the author in compiling the first part of his work.

The material that has been drawn from this and other sources for compilation of the first part of the book has been ruthlessly condensed, in the knowledge that the working of the present-day machine is of far greater interest. Well-known incidents like that of the activities and trial of Casement, the better-known work of Mata Hari, the sensational woman spy whose cleverness has been written and pictured as real genius, have been merely mentioned: to all for whom the subject has real interest, these things would be mere redundancies. Such things as the trials of Schulz and Ernst could not be omitted, for they show the workings of the old system: they have been summarized as much as is possible, with clarity ever in view.

But, from the time of the formation of the Gestapo—from 1918 onward, in fact, no effort has been spared in making the record as complete and accurate as possible. Nothing has been said about British or French counter measures: it is not in the public interest that any reference should be made to these, other than by qualified authorities, and thus, if the statements made here should appear to show German espionage as superior to anything else in the world, so it must stand. As now constituted, it is very good indeed: whether it is quite good enough remains to be seen.

Some of the statements concerning Gestapo

work, as they appear in this book, may and probably will be challenged. Time will prove that not one of them exceeds the truth. In more than one instance they are utterly at variance with the commonly accepted accounts of events, but the accounts in question are no more than examples of the ingenuity of German propagandists, who have reduced lying to a very fine art indeed. As, in the second part of this work—incidentally, also in the first part—will speedily appear.

Authorities in support of Part I have been quoted above. Obviously, at this present time, the author's sources of information for the second part cannot be revealed—yet. Again, time will prove their genuineness.

Finally, in support of what is written here; I have quoted a few authorities in support of Part I of this work. I know that a spate of "German spy" and other books have appeared in consequence of the never-ending "Crisis" (and was ever a word so much abused?) and the subsequent war, but I aver, on my honour, that I have not looked at, let alone read, one of them. Thus, if I trench on their preserves, it is in utter ignorance. I would say, both as regards that one point, and as concerning this book as a whole, with one of old—"By Him who sleeps at Abouthis, I write the truth."

PHILIP ST. C. WALTON-KERR
London,
   October 9th, 1939.

Part I

Stieber's System: *circa* 1847 to 1918

I

KARL STIEBER

A PAIR of spies crossed the Jordan and managed to get into Jericho without detection by the garrison: they managed to get in touch with a woman who was willing to aid her country's enemies, and promised her protection in return for her services. Quite probably she gave them a good deal of useful information as to the strength of the place, the dispositions of its garrison, and the state of the country generally, as nearly as she knew it. Still more probably, a woman of her profession knew a great deal, for the clients of such a one would come to her in their unguarded moments, most likely under the influence of drink, and with loose tongues.

The spies took back a quantity of useful information, economic, topographic, and military. When the main body of the attackers crossed the Jordan and captured Jericho, Rahab, the harlot, was protected as had been promised, and even, it appears, rewarded for the useful work she had done. Thus the first historic case of espionage has a woman in it, probably as attractive a figure as the woman spy of fiction.

From her day onward, espionage of a sort figures in all military operations, but not until the time of Napoleon was it systematized and recognized as an important branch of military operations. Prior to his time, however, the Venetian Republic had established a system rather akin to that on which the Russian Ogpu works, a secret supervision of economic and political life which, perhaps, has never been excelled in thoroughness. In that system, all was written, nothing spoken: German commercial espionage is modelled on it.

There is a historic parallel for every activity of the modern German espionage system, even to the use of minorities for the destruction of neighbouring states. When Cortes began his Aztec campaign, he seduced and made his mistress the daughter of a cacique, to whom the name Marina was given, and of whom it was said that she had the melancholy distinction of having done more than any other person toward rivetting the chains of the conquerors on her unfortunate countrymen. Through her, Cortes learned of the dissensions in and about Montezuma's Aztec empire, and he made use of them, fostered and increased discontent among the Tlascalans, a powerful tribe of the Mexican plateau, until he was able to make them his allies and so conquer the empire in which he had sown dissensions in addition to those already existing. Tlascala forms a very good parallel to Sudetenland.

But, in all these historic examples, work was sporadic, organized for the needs of the moment, and discontinued as soon as the need had passed. Napoleon laid down rules, organized espionage as a permanent part of his military system, and so formed the model on which, later, Germany shaped its adjunct to world-conquest, mainly through the genius of one man, Karl Stieber.

He was a native of Mersebourg, a Saxon town, and was born toward the end of the second decade of last century. His parents belonged to the professional class, and were able to give him a good education—not so easy a matter in those days as now—and carry it on until he eventually qualified as a barrister. As nearly as is known, he was no great success in that profession; in 1847 he abandoned it to take a post in a great manufacturing concern in Silesia, and, at first, appeared to throw himself heart and soul into the Socialistic activities which, even then, were beginning to appear as a threat to Prussian aristocracy.

He was then nearly thirty years of age. Trusted by the local leaders of the Socialist movement, he kept in with the employing class to such an extent that he captured the affections of the daughter of one of the directors of his firm, and so far involved the girl's uncle—another director—in Socialistic activities as to procure his arrest and a year's imprisonment for plotting against the Government and fomenting revolutionary movements among the employees of the firm.

It transpired much later that Stieber himself had done all of which his wife's uncle was accused, and then had denounced the man and produced plausible evidence against him. For the time being, Stieber remained apparently one of the leaders of the Socialist movement; in reality, he had already been given a post in the police service, and had begun his career as a secret agent.

By 1848, Socialism had—from the Prussian Government's point of view—made dangerous headway; all over Europe revolutionary tendencies were apparent. Demonstrations in Berlin evinced the power of the movement and the wakening of the working classes, and, working in his secret way on the side of the Government, Stieber made himself so useful that his activities came to the notice of the King of Prussia. Two more years of

Socialism's growth convinced the Prussian Government that strong repressive measures were necessary: Stieber, now a trusted and important figure in the police service, was appointed *Polizeirath*, a post which rendered him independent of all ordinary police control, and by virtue of which he was able to organize the system which endured until 1918. Based on the Napoleonic model, constructed throughout by the genius of Karl Stieber, the system included economic, political, and military espionage. In 1914, the admitted expenditure on this service was £780,000; how much beyond that amount was being spent by the diplomatic and political branches of the service is not, and probably never will be, known.

The organization of the military branch of Stieber's work presented many difficulties, only overcome by his use of the royal patronage that had been extended to him. Prussian military authorities had no liking for this ferrety outsider with his utter lack of reverence for their cherished theories; he was, to them, nothing but a common informer, and he had to use all his tact, and all the power given him, to proceed in spite of prejudice. The police, too, hated him: they had no control over his actions, although his work was—in their view— merely a branch of their own. Both services regarded him as an upstart, and one, at that, who indulged in dirtier, more underhand practices than they were prepared to countenance. Yet, shielded by his royal patron, and getting results all the time from his work, Stieber set up and perfected his organization, accessory both to the regular police force and the army, but responsible to neither.

There was a political and Court side to the organization, too, and Stieber's *Memoirs* give far

more details of this than of his other activities.
King Frederick William of Prussia was deeply interested in the sayings and doings of Court personages, and Stieber kept him well supplied with
reports—mere tittle-tattle, for the most part, but
interesting enough to assure him full protection and
independence in his work. Thus he organized a
secret police which covered all of Prussia, so
thoroughly that nobody was free of its activities.
So thorough was it, in fact, that agitation against
him grew to an extent which in the end compelled
him to resign his post; by that time, though, he had
other interests which rendered him quite willing to
resign: his work in Prussia itself was finished; the
machine he had built could run, now, independently of his control.

In 1854, with a grant of over £12,000 to cover his
expenses, he began the establishment of Prussian
espionage in neighbouring countries. Bismarck,
then at the beginning of his career, aimed at raising
Prussia to the status of a first-class European power,
and envisaged a war or two as necessary to his plans.
He had not then—perhaps he never had—the
vision of world-conquest on which Germany
wrecked an Empire in 1914–18; Prussian in essence,
he saw Prussia as master of all Germans, and
realized that vision when the German Empire was
formed: Hohenzollern ambition went the rest of the
way, and paid the penalty: the old man at Doorn
knows all that story.

Bismarck saw in Stieber the tool he wanted, and
used that tool in every possible way. It does not
appear that Stieber had much to do with the
Schleswig-Holstein affair; probably, as was the case
with Himmler and his Gestapo over the Danzig
farce, Stieber held a watching brief, and the active

work which he and his secret police were later to do in other quarters was not needed in the Danish affair. Already Bismarck had his eye on Austria, and there Stieber was needed, and was set to work with a view to making the outcome of the Austrian campaign a German—or rather Prussian— success before Bismarck began hostilities. The result showed the wisdom of the Iron Chancellor.

How Stieber conducted his pre-war campaign he is careful not to tell in those *Memoirs* of his. He was a born psychologist, as at this time are so many of the Gestapo chiefs: he chose his men and placed them—he had years in which to complete the work —so well that when, in 1866, Prussia moved against Austria, there was not a village on the line of route, let alone a town, that had not its informer waiting to give the Prussian troops all the information available as to the numbers and dispositions of the Austrian troops, their sources of supply, their routes and movements—everything that communications of that time could provide. Stieber had half-conquered the Austrian forces; the task of the Prussian army was merely the other half, and the one battle of Sadowa concluded the campaign— Austria was defeated there beyond retrieving. Over this, Stieber was created "Chief of the Active Service Police." There had been no such force before: he made it, and with four years intervening between that time and the first Franco-Prussian war, he more than justified its existence.

During those four years, the "fixed posts" which had proved of such value in the Austrian campaign were extended to north-eastern France, as preparation for the war which Bismarck had planned for the extension of Prussian domination.

By "fixed post" was indicated a spy in Prussian pay: the French police and municipal authorities of that time paid little or no attention to the immigration of a German hairdresser, butcher, baker, or other small independent trader to town or village; this system of planting spies was new, unrecognized, and the German (not always German, even, for Stieber used all nationalities, even including French subjects willing to act against their country) who came to settle always had good reason for establishing himself in the chosen spot. Very seldom indeed were these agents employees; usually they set up in a business of some sort, made friends in the locality, and then set to work to collect every kind of information for transmission to Berlin. Nothing was neglected; the habits and foibles of individuals, especially those of the official classes, were docketed and indexed at Stieber's headquarters; all the area over which Prussian troops might operate was surveyed and mapped, so that when war broke out in 1870 the Prussians knew the terrain as well as or better than the French themselves, knew its possibilities of supply and the difficulties they might encounter at any given point. Every fortification was accurately located and described: the work as a whole was a complete military reconnaissance of enemy country, while as yet the France of Napoleon III failed to envisage a Prussian war.

Bismarck, all this time, was busy detaching France from its possible friends in Europe, so that, when war came, the nation he intended to humiliate and lessen should stand utterly alone. Stieber had been made privy councillor after his work for the Sadowa campaign, and now was completely in the Chancellor's confidence. If his *Memoirs* are to be believed, he was responsible for the breach between France and Russia, which Bismarck had striven to bring about.

He states that, on the occasion of the Czar Alexander's visiting the Emperor Napoleon, he ascertained that a military review at Longchamps, at which both sovereigns would take the salute, was to be the occasion of an attempt on the Czar's life. He transmitted this information to Bismarck, who conceived the idea of letting the attempt take place, but frustrating it and capturing the would-be assassin. Under French law, Bismarck knew well, a merely attempted crime would not bring capital punishment to the offender, and Alexander would remember that his assailant had been let off lightly. And so it happened: when Prussia eventually made war on France, and Napoleon looked to Russia for aid of some sort, he looked in vain: the Longchamps incident had ruined all chances of a Franco-Russian alliance.

Whether the privy councillor and master spy had any part in the affair of the Ems telegram is not known. Bismarck, determined on war with France, had tried to bring about a rupture over the offer of the Spanish throne to Prince Leopold of Hohenzollern, but the King of Prussia, then over seventy years of age and a lover of peace, composed the difficulty. He knew France would not permit a Hohenzollern to rule in Spain, and persuaded Leopold to refuse the offer, to Bismarck's utter disgust, since there was now no cause for war.

The old King of Prussia went to Ems to take the cure, while the Chancellor took his holiday at his country seat, where he invited von Moltke and von Roon, the former of whom subsequently commanded the Prussian forces in the field, to join him. All three were very depressed; Bismarck had determined to resign his post; the two generals wished they could do the same, since, after making certain that the army was completely ready, they were deprived of their war. At the height of their gloom the telegram which was later to become famous arrived: according to Bismarck's memoirs, they were at dinner at the time, and he opened the telegram and read it to his two guests.

It stated that the French Ambassador, at Ems, had sought an assurance from the King of Prussia that under no circumstances would he support a Hohenzollern claim or candidature to the Spanish throne. To this the King had replied that Prince Leopold's claim had been withdrawn, and therefore he regarded the matter as concluded. As far as the future was concerned, naturally, he could not give such an indefinite guarantee as the French Ambassador had asked, and he saw no necessity for it, or for any further meeting for discussion of the subject.

In its original form, the telegram was innocuous enough: the Ambassador had made a courteous request, and the King had given him an equally courteous reply to the effect that the request was unnecessary. Neither the Prussian King nor the French people desired war: Napoleon the Little, it is true, was clanking his sword and boasting of France's readiness, but France itself was inclined to peace. Bismarck, determined on war, studied the inoffensive telegram, took a pencil, and began a series of careful deletions. When he had finished, the text of the message gave the impression that the French Ambassador had flung out a demand which amounted to an insult, and that the King of Prussia had not only refused the demand, but had forbidden the Ambassador to seek any further interviews with him.

Bismarck read the telegram in its new form to his two cronies, who instantly recovered from their depression. "Our God of old lives yet," said von Roon. "He will not let us perish in disgrace." Von Moltke was equally enthusiastic, and together with Bismarck they drank to the war on which all three were determined. The next day, practically every newspaper in Europe reproduced Bismarck's version of the telegram, and war between the two nations became inevitable.

Commentators of the period ascribed the rapid Prussian success in great measure to the superiority of the "needle-gun," the Prussian rifle, over the French infantry arm. Not until Stieber's *Memoirs* were published did it appear that the defeats suffered by the French were due in greater degree to the disclosure of their strategy to the enemy, for whom a "fixed post" was waiting with full information at every step of their advance. As in the Sadowa campaign, fully half the work had been done before hostilities began, and neither France nor any other country had any idea of the existence of such an organization as Stieber had built up: it was something utterly new, a Prussianly thorough adaptation and improvement on Napoleon's military espionage; it was meanly, dirtily despicable, and, achieving the desired results at the time, it so far modified the whole Prussian character that lying and trickery are essentials in what passes for modern German diplomacy. The 1914 "scrap of paper," the series of broken promises, aggressions, and injustices which have again led to war in September of 1939—all these violations of humanity's natural and unescapeable laws are directly traceable to the Stieber principle that the end justifies any means, fraud and crime equally with honesty.

With the formation of the German Empire, Stieber's career reached its climax. Up to that point his work had been personal; he had organized his ''fixed posts'' in Austria and France, selected his agents with the almost uncanny power of sizing up their fitness that was his, and spent the grants devoted to his work so wisely that Prussia honoured him for his great cunning and his unscrupulous services. After '71, the work was no longer personal. Espionage had become a department, with Stieber as its head—just such a figure as one sees in "gang" mystery stories, where the Spider, or the Hooded Cobra, or Alpha or the Crimson Cross sits at the centre of a system of crookdom and directs his agents to rob a bank or murder a financier. He was far more cunning, far more clear-sighted, than the majority of these villains of fiction; he knew men and women as few know them, and he had an un-German appreciation of Latin mentalities. In that he was unique; German attempts at world domination have so far failed because the German, and especially the Prussian, is unable to grasp the points of view of other nations, but sees the whole world through German spectacles. Why, the Nazi asks at this present time, should not other nations be willing to follow on the path opened up by our glorious German youth, and accept the Nazi ideal in order that all mankind may be regenerated, Germanized, bent to harmony with the Fuehrer's will? Stieber knew mankind better, and when Kaiser Wilhelm dropped the pilot, let Bismarck pass to private life, Stieber too became a nonentity, to die in 1892 and rank as an honoured figure in the accomplishment of German aims. From the Prussian standpoint, he had done well.

One aspect of his work, one that has been very

carefully carried on by his successors, is even at this time not realized to the full: it is the use of industrial unrest against an enemy. Stieber grew up into the Socialist and Syndicalist movements which, originating in the desire of the working classes for betterment, produced in Germany Karl Marx and the beginnings of what is now Communism. At the outset, Stieber used the movement for his own advantage, betrayed his wife's uncle to the Government and became a secret agent for constituted authority among the would-be rebels against it. Later, he saw how what is now known as the Communist movement might be used to the advantage of Prussia, and his successors have seen how valuable a weapon it is in the struggle for world-domination. A few instances will illustrate the point: one might have been accidental; two might have been coincidences, but the series is irrefutable evidence of the Prussian will to conquest at any cost, including the use of sincere idealists to further aims of which they have no conception.

As far back as 1893 (this concerns German secret service as a whole, for by that time Stieber himself was dead) the German Government voted a credit of 80,000 thalers, to pay the expenses of "foreign publications useful to the policy of the Empire." Almost immediately after this, there appeared in France a slim booklet known as the *Mesnard Pamphlet*, which was addressed to the railwaymen of France. It anticipated the workers' councils of Russia, of over a quarter of a century later, by carrying Republicanism on to Bolshevism. "The employees," said the pamphlet, "should themselves elect their chiefs in accordance with the principle of universal suffrage. It would be merely logical if the employees should choose those who might give them orders, and should turn out those who proved unjust or incapable.

"The last resource of railway workers in search of justice is a strike. A strike is a legitimate weapon, and the fact cannot be controverted. If it is suppressed, its suppression constitutes an abuse of the powers of the stronger party. With the organization which the syndicate (of workers) cannot fail to possess in a short time, we shall have arrived at a position from which we can contemplate the possibility of a general strike on all the railways, and in similar organizations if necessary. It is very important that everybody should consider this problem. No partial strikes, but patience, and in the end a general strike."

With this incitement to defiance, the authors of the pamphlet foresaw that mobilization of the French Army might nullify their efforts: they tried to provide against this by telling French railwaymen that mobilization for the prevention of a strike would not affect them. The authors of the pamphlet professed themselves railwaymen so far as to say—

"We know our duty as patriots, and we know when we must be soldiers, but if you gentlemen, you officers, do not know it, then leave us to manage our own affairs: otherwise, we shall call in the Prussians."

"Mesnard," obviously a section of the foreign propaganda department organized by Stieber in the first place, was trying to incite the railwaymen of France to strike and refuse military service at a juncture critical in French affairs. It was openly stated by a French railwaymen's leader that the pamphlet constituted a German attempt to establish influence over French workers—it was too clumsy, and defeated its own object. Stieber, by that time,

was dead: had he been alive, he would have worked
more subtly, not declared his hand to an extent
which revealed the object of the effort.

The pamphlet itself was distributed from Geneva,
which served as one of the principal headquarters
of the German secret service at that time. It has
been well said that Switzerland is the least neutral
of countries: it was at that time the residence of one
of the chief officials of the German espionage
system, and to this day, outwardly favouring
Britain for the sake of the tourist traffic, Switzerland is headquarters for every type of espionage
activity: centrally situated, ostensibly an utterly
neutral country, home of the League of Nations,
Switzerland is home of every agency of disruption.
Certain sealed railway carriages took Lenin and his
fellow plotters to Russia in the dark days of the
Kerensky Government. Whence?

A general strike—this is piling up instance into
coincidence—was declared in France at the time of
the Dreyfus trial, which at one point threatened
another war between Germany and France. The
strike proved anything but general: Stieber was
dead, and his successors had not his genius for
organization of the Latin peoples. Then again the
industrial weapon was put to use when, as warning
of what was to come, the Agadir affair showed that
peace could not be maintained, German ambition
being what it was. Coincidently with the Agadir
trouble, there were labour troubles in England; desperate attempts were made to stir up trouble on the
French railways at the same time, and, had they
succeeded, 1914 would have been antedated a few
years. Railway paralysis in France at the critical
moment would have been invaluable, but it could
not be achieved: the workers' leaders would have

none of it: the German effort was too crude: to put that in another way, Stieber was no longer in existence, and no genius of like insight had arisen.

Nineteen fourteen brought further industrial unrest in France, for, in spite of the lessons of the war of '70–'71, the industrial part of the country, later to become the main theatre of military operations in the west, was thickly planted with "fixed posts" by the German secret service. As for England, it was confidently believed up to the outbreak of war that the Ulster troubles would prevent this country from joining in.

In 1918, the secret service that Stieber had so well organized collapsed with the downfall of Prussianism, and French and British labour troubles, especially those of 1921 and 1926, may possibly be ascribed to other influences from outside the countries concerned. Yet, even then, defeated Germany was in some measure planning for recovery: the antipathy to Bolshevism that was to come later was not then evident; such German agents as assisted in producing unrest may have been in Russian pay, or may have been financed from Berlin. That they existed is beyond question.

As a final instance, the attempt at paralysing British railways by a strike at the end of August 1939, may be cited, though it belongs to the story of the modern German espionage organization rather than to that of the machinery which Stieber set up. It is proof that economic penetration of potential enemy countries is still a vital part of the German system, in which, even more to-day than in Bismarck's time, the end justifies any means.

It has been well said of Karl Stieber that, although he served his country to the limit of his abilities, his place is among the criminals and perverts of the world, not among its great men. The effect of his work is evident in the German character to-day, in the chicanery and double-dealing which is so prominent a feature of Nazi rule.

II

MILITARY ESPIONAGE: 1870–1918

OPEN invasion of France by Prussia began late in July of 1870. In reality, the invasion had begun three years earlier, and, when von Moltke's army began to move, there were already no less than 30,000 Prussian agents of Stieber's service resident in the departments of northern and eastern France. Through their aid, von Moltke's staff knew every move of the French forces as soon as it was made; often moves were made known to Prussian leaders before they were made, and this efficient espionage rendered inevitable the disaster of Sedan and the fall of Paris.

The surrender of the capital was made by Jules Favre, who began negotiations with Bismarck in 1871. The Chancellor sent for Stieber, and ordered him to keep watch on Favre until the terms were settled. In order to negotiate, Favre went to a house ostensibly belonging to a loyal Parisian, and situated in the Boulevard du Roi at Versailles. There he was hospitably received—the carriage in which he arrived had been driven by one of Stieber's men— and was recommended to make use of the services of a personal attendant capable of every service he might require, one who presented the highest credentials. Stieber tells this story in his *Memoirs*: the house in the Boulevard du Roi was the headquarters of the Prussian active service police; the personal attendant was Stieber himself.

The owner of the house was a clever and fully trusted member of the "fixed post" system, and knew all Versailles from end to end. Here, while discussions for the surrender went on, Favre stayed. Stieber waited on him at meals, took charge of his bedroom and personal belongings—and went through his pockets and baggage with a thoroughness born of long practice. Whether, as Stieber claims, the result of his activities was of vast assistance to the Chancellor in settling the terms of surrender is open to doubt: the master-spy was a vain man, as his *Memoirs* show, and inclined to claim credit on every possible occasion. But the incident goes to show that Bismarck was taking no chances, and perhaps he did benefit from his hound's nosing.

Then, after the end of the war, the necessity for continuance of the watch on France was realized. Stieber laid down definite rules for the organization of the service that continued to exist up to 1914— and, outside the occupied areas, to the end of the war in 1918. A few quotations from these rules define the duties of the agents:

"The fixed agents must not merely hold salaried posts (that is, in offices, workshops, and the like) for they might at any time be dismissed from their posts, and in that case would no longer have good reasons for remaining at their posts of observation. Such positions, also, would possess considerable disadvantages for our agents, since they would restrict actions and restrain them from freedom in coming and going, while bringing them too much under observation.

"Thus it must be stated that, as condition of the employment of an agent, that he shall be obliged to keep some sort of an establishment which he may

choose as long as it is, externally in any case, fully
in keeping with the commercial or other requirements of the country in which he is employed.
Whatever establishment it may be, whether an
office for the settlement of disputed claims (sic) or a
property register, or a business of commercial sort,
such as a grocery, a café, restaurant, hotel, etc., it
must be soundly established and be possessed of an
unquestionable goodwill.

"It must be understood that it is necessary for our
agents to inspire confidence in circles where their
centre of action lies, and to establish that confidence by outward declaration of an ordinary bourgeois existence; by discreet charity, and by making
themselves useful in societies, associations, communities, and the like; by acquiring definite social
positions, in order that they may be well received
and well regarded in all quarters.

"Whilst we must put limits to the expense which
our agents are permitted to incur, it is necessary that
they should be given an absolute assurance that any
deficit incurred in the conduct of the undertaking
which they carry on will be made good by the service under the head of general expenses of the
service."

These "fixed posts" were controlled from Brussels,
Lausanne, and Geneva, all cities of distinctly cosmopolitan character, and the salaries of the agents
were paid from those centres. Then, as check on
the work of the "fixed posts," a system of travelling
inspectorships was organized; ostensibly, the in-
spectors were commercial travellers representing
German firms, for the most part, though women
were also used for this type of work. They would
drop in at a "fixed post" at irregular intervals, collect
reports, and issue instructions. The pay for a "fixed

post" ranged between £2 and £5 a week, and the inspecting system assured that the main head-quarters at Berlin, to which all reports were eventually transmitted, got value for its money.

In addition to this main army, which at the outbreak of war in 1914 was known to consist of nearly 16,000 agents settled and paid in this way, fourteen of the French departments—those which Germany intended to occupy at the outbreak of war—had among their population some 4,000 agriculturalists, mainly labourers, and 5,000 to 6,000 women servants, who were maintained from headquarters until they secured employment, mostly among the official classes. All these were subsidiary to and under control of the "fixed posts"; their business was to make themselves self-supporting as soon as possible (if they failed to do this in a given time, they were either recalled or left to their own resources) and then to transmit information to such "fixed posts" as were made known to them, being paid solely by results.

The "fixed posts," or superior agents in permanent pay, were by no means of German origin in every case, though mostly they were recruited from some one of the Teutonic races. So far as the small fry under their rank was concerned, every German in a foreign country might be regarded as a spy of sorts, since he or she was certainly in touch— (whether knowingly or ignorantly) with a paid agent, and thus able to transmit intelligence of more or less value. Berlin neglects nothing, as will appear more and more plainly, and information which is, on the face of it, of no use whatever may be twisted to essential use.

To illustrate the military side of the organization, a "fixed post" in the vicinity of a French garrison or military post (English too, for that matter) may be defined. The agent establishes himself in a business of some sort: tobacco and newspapers, delicatessen, estate agency, dry goods or grocery—whatever it may be, in good times or bad times he is there, soundly established and carrying on, always keeping his end up, and a thoroughly good fellow. He is interested in social activities, able to contribute a bit to the local hospital and help toward making the church bazaar a success, and by his unostentatious goodness—not to mention his willingness to buy the other fellow a drink if they meet in the local hostelry—he very soon makes friends. Very capably bi-lingual, he betrays little or no trace of foreign origin, and, if there is any trace, he accounts for it so plausibly as to obviate suspicion. He is open in conversation, more anxious than willing to give account of himself, and, eventually, he manages to rank as a friend of some member of the garrison or other establishment of military significance. He may rank with the officers, or may be *persona grata* in the sergeants' mess; he may even provide funds for some frequenter of the men's canteen—and, whatever his standing, he poses as entirely ignorant of military significances. In reality, he has been trained in everything from gun calibres to commissariat sources, and not one word that is let fall is without its significance for him. He is dangerous from the word go, the more so because of his apparent ignorance, which induces talk on technical matters, and explanation of them by the loose-tongued, in the belief that his interest is mild and needs arousing. In all this he is perfectly trained before being appointd to his post, and he is, above all, a most friendly soul.

Now—and this applies to every country—no man

is so happy as when he can talk shop, and display his knowledge to the uninitiate. The "fixed post" agent trades on this: he does not mind arguing, giving in gracefully, and being convinced of exactly where and how he is wrong—and he is regarded as more than ever a good fellow for submitting to correction. The result of the argument goes down in his report, and eventually reaches Berlin: the guns in so-and-so casemate are not 4.7, but five-inch, and the battery is capable of so-and-so rounds per minute, range so-and-so, and observation posts at such-and-such. All that as result of a little argument and, possibly, a few drinks, which go down as expenses for the travelling inspector to pay.

After a while, the agent forms intimacies, gets admitted to household circles; takes a hand at bridge for an evening, perhaps. Eventually, he wins some woman's confidence, and begins to collect personal details of members of the post to which he is allotted. Headquarters tabulates the information he sends in, checks it with that obtained from other sources, and piles up a mass of detail which may or may not be eventually useful. Much of it is common knowledge which might be obtained with no difficulty or expense, but, in the view of the chiefs of military espionage, absolute certainty on all points is necessary, and only by the use of trained agents can this be assured.

A very good instance of the value of this thoroughness is provided by the fate of the fortress of Maubeuge at the time of the German advance on Paris in 1914. It was regarded as—and probably was —able to withstand anything short of accurate fire from the heaviest type of siege guns, which, before they can be used, must be mounted on platforms specially constructed to take the strain imposed in

firing such guns. Maubeuge fell in about a tenth of
the time necessary for the construction of such
platforms, because, about four miles distant from
the fortifications, an agent of the firm of Krupp had
bought and enclosed some 700 acres in the Forest of
Lanieres, ostensibly for the establishment of a locomotive factory. This transaction had been carried
through in 1911, and, in addition to putting up a
locomotive factory, the firm constructed platforms
on which its own type of siege guns and giant
howitzers could be mounted, so as totally to silence
the defensive armament of the forts.

This was not all: thanks to the agents planted in
and about Maubeuge, the German artillery commanders knew the position, bore, rate of fire of the
guns they had to silence, and the composition of
the forces working them. They knew where best to
site their own artillery for fire effect and immunity
from the French guns, and for every big howitzer
and gun placed in position, a platform of the right
type was ready. Maubeuge was the most striking
instance of this pre-war espionage and preparation:
Namur furnished an almost similar illustration of
the perfect thoroughness of these agents' work; it,
too, fell almost without halting the advance of the
German masses.

The agent's work includes every detail of the
locality in which he is placed. The qualities and
capabilities for bearing traffic of roads; sites, vulner-
ability, and composition of bridges; location of telegraph, telephone, and power wires; positions and
depths at all seasons of fords; extent and availability
for use of every farm and building; food supplies;
numbers of motor vehicles—from cycles to heavy
lorries—locations of garages and probable supplies
of petrol: not a detail is missed, and it is well said

that both France and England are better known to
the authorities in Berlin than to their own people.
This is as true to-day as it was in the first and second
decades of the century. In the event of a German advance, every officer has maps and instructions which
enable him to move with just as much certainty as,
say, on the parade ground where he was drilled.

The training of these "fixed post" agents is a
serious business, and no one of them is allotted to a
post until he has passed certain examinations; he
must be able to report on guns and men, engineering and topographical details, correctly, since any
errors in his information would render it all useless.
He is usually such an efficient surveyor as to be able
to draw up plans of ground merely from observation, or with no more than the aid of photographs.
A good instance of this is provided by the agent
who was set to report on the Forth Bridge, with a
view to its destruction at any set time: he had to
furnish details of the construction of the bridge
itself, and state how the men engaged to destroy it
should be placed; he had to report on the geology
of the district, the depth and nature of the bridge's
foundations, and the amounts of various sorts of
explosive, possible to transport to the spot, that
would be required to make a complete job of it.
Nineteen-twentieths of all this information was
available in ordinary books of reference; photographs of the bridge from every point and in every
aspect are available, most of them as picture post-
cards, but Berlin wanted the whole thing checked
by one of their own men. He was arrested before
his work was completed, and such details as he
had had to put on paper, since they were too
intricate for him to commit them to memory,
proved amazingly accurate.

As in actual war, so in military espionage—the
agent is never faced by identical circumstances a
second time, and thus he has to adapt himself,
make use of accident, and, most of all, judge the
men with whom he comes in contact so as to make
the best use of them. To a certain extent his value
decreases as soon as open war begins, but German
agents, who have resided at their posts long enough
to be regarded as normal citizens, have their value
all the time. Movements of troops may be learned
and transmitted; women especially are injudicious
over such things, and husbands are often indiscreet.
Men on leave congregate in bars and cafés, and—
inevitably—talk shop. A word dropped here and
another there, and the agent has a story for headquarters, and his own ways of transmitting it.

It is a mean game, one of gaining and betraying
confidences, abusing the hospitality of the country
and people to which the agent has gained access.
Germany perfected it, goes on using it, and will go
on elaborating and using it so long as the Prussian
conception of life and ethics continues to exist.
That a man of any nationality should risk his freedom in time of peace, in order to gain purely military information, is conceivable; that he should
worm his way into the confidence of a community
on the lines laid down by Stieber, and betray that
confidence, is Prussian: there is a difference between
the two.

III

THE SCHULZ AND ULLMO CASES

IN the early days of the war which began in 1914,
three British cruisers, the *Aboukir*, *Cressy*, and
Hogue, were torpedoed and sunk by a single enemy
submarine. It was a neat piece of work, complicated only by the presence, in the vicinity of the
sinkings, of a trawler, of which not even the
nationality, let alone the name and port of registry,
was ever ascertained. A little, innocent-looking
trawler. . . .

A justifiable piece of camouflage and aid to submarine operations, concerning which no complaint
can be made. An instance of espionage work which
any sailor-man would countenance, for a submarine
faces tremendous odds in attacking not merely one,
but three cruisers, and, doubtless, the trawler supplemented such surface information as the periscope
of a submarine of that day could obtain. Had the
trawler been as innocent as it looked, it would have
turned up again somewhere with particulars of the
sinkings. It did not, as far as British or French
ports were concerned.

Prior to the outbreak of war, two cases stand out
as typical of German naval espionage: they are the
Schulz trial in England, and the case of Lieutenant
Ullmo and the siren who ruined him, in France.
The Schulz case may first be considered as typical of
the work of the naval spy and the very large funds
put at his disposal for the accomplishment of his

40

aims: Ullmo's tragedy—for it is no less—ranks more nearly among the romances of espionage, goes to show how a man may sacrifice his career and even his honour at a woman's bidding.

Dr. Max Schulz was arraigned at the Devon Assizes after committal from police court proceedings, on four charges. Firstly, that in 1911 "he, at the borough of Plymouth, having possession of or control over knowledge which had been obtained by means of an act which constituted an offence against the Official Secrets Act, communicated or attempted to communicate to a person to whom the same ought not in the interests of the State to be communicated at the time."

The second charge was virtually a fuller statement of the first, in that it defined the recipient or intended recipient of the information Schulz had gained as the Government of a foreign State. Quite apart from the normal practice in such cases, there was no need to specify that State. Two more charges went to show that Schulz "endeavoured to procure Samuel Hugh Duff and Edward Charles Tarrant respectively to communicate to him information relating to the naval affairs of His Majesty, which ought not in the interests of the State to be communicated to any person."

Since every other German of the professional class is either "Herr Doktor" or "Herr Professor," Schulz's right to the title he claimed is of little consequence. Evidence against him went to show that he practised no profession but that of a spy, after his arrival in the British Isles. He began work in Ireland, went thence to Toulon, and did little beyond making himself conspicuous in either place. By 1911 he was in Plymouth, still thirsting for information, and with enough funds to go yachting: during a brief cruise up the River Yealm, he got in touch with Duff and Tarrant, who, giving evidence against him at his trial, were both able to prove that they were in no way implicated in his activities, which were directed toward obtaining naval information.

The case, forgotten now, aroused nation-wide interest at the time. Sir Rufus Isaacs, Attorney-General of that day, led for the Crown. It was divulged that Schulz had offered Duff no less than £500 a year, and had also offered to pay Tarrant £50 a month, if they would supply him with information concerning naval affairs and personages. This, he said, was to be published in a German newspaper of which he was correspondent. Papers found in Schulz's possession showed that he was supplied with funds from abroad by a certain Tobler, who issued instructions from time to time. Some of these, as read in court from letters found in Schulz's possession, are definite, if rather elementary. One outlines the information required concerning unnamed persons:

"How do matters stand between the commander and the lieutenant respectively? Can nothing at all be expected from them? Reserve officers are of no use: they do not procure any valuable secrets because they do not have access to them. Confidential reports and books are what are wanted, and what you must procure at all costs if our relations are to continue."

It appeared that Schulz's work did not give satisfaction, and that the "relations" became rather strained at times. Schulz used to send telegrams to Tobler in code: the key was discovered, and the telegrams read in court. One said—"In greatest danger. Wire immediately £50." Whether Tobler complied with the request was not stated, but probably he did not, since another message was still more urgent: "In greater trouble and danger. All prepared for departure. Wire immediately £50 and date of meeting." From which it would appear that the sums expended on naval espionage went far beyond those allowed the military branch.

Schulz communicated to Tobler the possibilities arising out of his getting in touch with Duff, and immediately received the following orders, defining the nature of the information required:

"Are officers or men granted leave, or have those on leave been possibly recalled?

"Is there any sign of coals, stores, ammunition, etc., being accumulated? What is the feeling in naval circles? How do officers and men discuss the situation?

"Are crews being increased, are ships being prepared, or has commissioning of ships suddenly taken place?

"What is the opinion of officers of the British Navy as to the result of war between England and France on the one hand, and Germany on the other, and the likelihood of the same over the Moroccan question?

"What ships of the Third Division were put out of service on July 23rd, or about the end of July, or have reduced their crews, and the reasons for so doing? How many officers and men are still on board, and why was the programme altered after it had been stated that the Third Division should be full up?"

Perusal of these questions convinced Duff that the German newspaper of which Schulz had spoken was a myth, and, in spite of Schulz's offer of £500 a year, Duff went straight to the police and told them

everything. Tarrant, in touch with Duff, did like-
wise. Schulz pleaded that he was a journalist and
nothing else, and had no intention of making im-
proper use of any information that might be given
him. But the plea was of no avail. The " Moroccan
question" over which one of Tobler's requests was
framed was at that time a possible source of danger,
and by the time the prosecution had fully stated its
case there could be no doubt as to Schulz's real
occupation. In view of the fact that he had accomplished nothing, he was given the comparatively
light sentence of a year and nine months in the
second division, and, having made himself too conspicuous to be of any further use to his German
employers, was totally ignored by them after his
release.

It is difficult at this time to understand the reason
for employing so clumsy and ineffective an agent, at
such a high rate of remuneration. Difficult, too, to
understand why Schulz retained so much incriminating evidence in his possession: instructions
to all such agents are to the effect that they must
memorize all instructions and then destroy them,
retaining no documents which may betray the
holder.

The case is interesting only in that it reveals the
methods pursued by the old German secret service,
and goes to show that in some cases the heads of
that service mistook their men and paid for ineffi-
ciency. The other case, that of Lieutenant Ullmo,
is more dramatic.

Ullmo was a sub-lieutenant of the French naval
service, and had been posted to the battleship
Carabine. He was a youngster of very attractive personality, well liked by his superiors and popular in
the wardroom of his ship. He had from the outset

proved himself a man of outstanding abilities, and appeared destined for a distinguished career when he became acquainted with a certain Mademoiselle Lison, and instantly fell for her charms. She was *petite*, blonde, piquante. A portrait reveals her face as not over-attractive in repose, but obviously capable of great charm of expression, and she had a dainty, perfect little figure. Ullmo's acquaintance with her very soon ripened to intimacy, and he lavished presents on her. His pay as a naval officer was meagre, but he had a private capital of nearly 80,000 francs—at pre-war rate of exchange, a little over £3,000—on which he drew from time to time to buy her favours.

Intimacy became infatuation: Mademoiselle tactfully showed him that she preferred him to his brother officers, as long as he was prepared to excel them in generosity: a lover in his position is easily inflamed to jealousy, and Lison played on that quality until she had persuaded him to acquire and furnish a large *appartement* for her use—and for his too, when his duties allowed it. The intimacy lasted two years, in which time Ullmo spent all his 80,000 francs on the lady, who, among other things, suggested raising more money by turning her establishment into an opium den for the benefit of Ullmo's brother officers. This was done, and still the income was not enough for her: Ullmo pointed out that he had given her everything and had no more, when in turn she pointed out that there were ways of raising money, and explained fully what she meant by it.

Ullmo was utterly indignant, and refused altogether to sacrifice his honour as an officer to his passion as a man. Lison coldly bade him farewell, knowing both him and the extent of his infatuation for her well enough to understand that he could not give her up. But, in order to force him to compliance with her wishes, she appeared about to instal a brother officer in his place, and with that he gave way. There were certain documents in a safe on board the *Carabine*, and Ullmo agreed to abstract them and hand them over to a person whom Lison would designate to him at an appointed time: in payment, he was to receive not merely the sums he had spent on the lady, but over half a million francs: this was a verbal promise, made by Lison herself.

But, she pointed out to him, she herself could not conclude the transaction. He had to arrange it with the other side by means of advertisements in certain newspapers, which he began to do. The phrasing of the advertisements brought them to the notice of a branch of the French Sûreté; they were decoded, Ullmo was traced by them, and eventually arrested. Since no evidence against Lison could be found, she was left at liberty, even when she appeared as a charming and only slightly interested spectator at her former lover's trial.

Ullmo, weak rather than bad, confessed everything. He was degraded from his rank and sentenced to life imprisonment—and, under French law, such a sentence literally means imprisonment until death, not a period of twenty years with remission for good conduct. Lison disappeared altogether after the trial: known as she was to the Sureté, she was of no more use to her German employers in France: possibly, under a different identity, she may have used her attractions in some other country to such ends as brought about Ullmo's downfall.

The story goes to show that attractive women

sometimes play parts in secret service activities, but they are employed far less than is popularly supposed. The mysterious siren of fiction is mainly mythical; she would attract too much attention to be useful, if she existed: Ullmo's case goes to show what a charming woman can do with a susceptible man, but it was an exceptional case.

Another, that of Mata Hari, has been told so many times, both in print and on the screen, that it is not worth repeating here. Similarly, and as an instance of naval espionage work, the Casement affair is too well known for repetition. Casement had done such good service in the Putumayo inquiry and similar things that he had been given a knighthood before 1914: implicated during the course of the war in dangerous activities, he faced a firing squad and so paid the ultimate penalty imposed on the spy. A sincere believer in the possibility of obtaining justice for Ireland through German aid, or a traitor to the country that had honoured him—what you will.

Other cases of naval espionage might be cited, but they would be merely variants of the Schulz affair. A case that comes to public notice is an example of failure on the part of the spy: the really outstanding, useful work never gets outside the archives of the British Special Branch, or the corresponding department of the French Sureté.

IV

DIPLOMACY'S BACKSTAIRS

THERE was, in those good old days before 1914, a separate organization of Court and diplomatic espionage in Germany, headed by a Colonel Baron von Tausch, who, like Stieber, went to such lengths that he made things too hot for himself. Unlike Stieber, who merely resigned his control of internal espionage to start work in neighbouring countries, von Tausch made things too dangerous altogether, and the Minister of Foreign Affairs of that day took counsel with his master, Wilhelm, who now enjoys privacy at Doorn, and, very much to Wilhelm's dismay, instituted proceedings against von Tausch, alleging libel and conspiracy. The whole affair throws a lurid light on Hohenzollern Court life, and shows up Wilhelm and his associates as very hot stuff indeed.

So many scandals came to light in the course of the trial that the whole German Court was alarmed over what might be revealed next. Nothing had been too mean or too small to escape entry in the Colonel Baron's dossier. Especially was this the case over Count Philip zu Eulenberg, who had been German Ambassador at the Viennese Court. Philip had been a sexual invert from his youth up: like many of that type, he had brains; like all of them, he had no morals. He served for quite a time as the Kaiser's colleague in degeneracy, for in his heyday

Wilhelm was a rip of rips—the records of the trial of von Tausch are enough to prove this. Certain clean-minded members of the Court tried to get Eulenberg ousted from the Imperial favour, but without avail. He had influence which could not be shaken—until von Tausch's trial revealed him for what he was. It put an end to his Court career. He had, it must be confessed, made quite a good ambassador at Vienna. While there, he had received a letter (produced at von Tausch's trial) in which the writer—von Tausch, of course—stated that he had done a piece of espionage work for which he might justly claim credit. He had managed to obtain information which would put an end to the influence of the German Foreign Minister, the letter stated, and he hoped that, by means of his information, the Minister would be forced to resign. The resignation duly took effect, whereupon Eulenberg secured for von Tausch the insignia of one of the highest Austrian orders, which was received with joy by one who was as vain of uniforms and decorations as Goering is to-day.

Another revelation of the trial was that von Tausch, acting under orders from Wilhelm II, had used despicable means to gain information about the nationalist organizations in Prussian Poland— Poland was not then an independent state, but was still partitioned between Germany, Austria, and Russia. Von Tausch selected a certain Baron von Lutzow, and sent him to Poland with orders to capture the heart of a daughter of a Polish noble who was a leader of the nationalist party. Von Lutzow was only too willing: he went to Poland— von Tausch, apparently, knew the type of man necessary for such an enterprise—and very soon won the girl's heart, establishing himself in her father's confidence. When he had secured the required information, and incidentally seduced the girl, he came back to impart all he had learned to von Tausch for the Kaiser's benefit. That he left behind a heartbroken girl was of no consequence whatever to the Hohenzollern gang.

Yet another vicious figure, Prince Egon Hohenlohe, was exposed by the trial. He, like Eulenberg, was a sexual invert, and thus one of Wilhelm II's pets, and also was intimately associated with the establishment of the Duke of Saxe-Coburg-Gotha. Over that, he took a violent dislike to one of the chamberlains of the Duke's Court, and called on von Tausch for aid in forcing the man from his place. Von Tausch set to work, and discovered that the unfortunate chamberlain had risen to his position from next to menial status. It was enough: the facts of the chamberlain's birth and connections were published in papers throughout Germany, and, although a capable and honest servant of the Court, he was compelled to resign his post— like the Foreign Minister.

Hohenlohe's reward for this piece of work was another order, which he wangled somehow. Other people discovered how useful a person was this secret policeman, and von Tausch, toward the end of his sticky career, used to appear at Court with rows of insignia decorating his more or less manly breast. He also sported the ribbons of his orders when the libel case opened, but the various revelations made in the first stages alarmed his imperial master. What would come to light next was not merely beyond telling, but terribly frightening; von Tausch knew so much that, had the case been carried to its conclusion, virtually every reputation in the German Court would have been ruined. He

was therefore dismissed from the case as under orders
by the Kaiser, who, naturally, was above the law.

A Bavarian Court of honour subsequently ad-
judged him guilty of conduct unbefitting one of his
rank, and stated that he was unfit for further service
in the Imperial Court. He was therefore turned out,
disgraced—and, by the orders of Wilhelm II, became a private gentleman with all the honours of a
retired diplomat, with a pension to enable him to
maintain his position. This was quite independent
of the monies he had obtained by blackmail and (as
an American might say) near-blackmail in his official position. He spent his declining years quite
comfortably, a more or less honoured figure in
German society. Quite a few members of that
society dared do no other than honour him.

In connection with Philip zu Eulenberg, the prosecution of Maximilian Harden, editor of the
German paper *Die Zukunft*, is illuminating as regards the quality of the Hohenzollern Court.
Harden, in a series of articles, had the courage to
show up Eulenberg as the degenerate he was and
always had been, and the prosecution was instigated with a view to maintaining Eulenberg in his
position as boy-friend of the Kaiser. Harden remarked—instead of making a studied defence—that
he had in his possession so much correspondence
as would blight the reputation of every member of
the Imperial family, and also would implicate most
of the high officers of the Court and of the Imperial
Guards. The prosecution was withdrawn, and *Die
Zukunft* went on being published. Harden was a
trifle more careful, naturally, but he had won his
point. From 1907 (the year of Harden's trial)
Eulenberg's influence over affairs was negligible
Possibly the Kaiser was growing too old. . . .

Such records of dirty usages, common to and recognized by the Prussian régime, lead one to dirty conclusions. They point, past question, to moral deterioration—in a normal, properly constituted society such a one as von Tausch would never have come to such power as he held and used. Moreover, the rottenness which his trial exposed would not have existed in a normal society, for average people, of any rank, have other interests than those of sexual abnormality. One harks back, instinctively, to Stieber, the genius who achieved Prussian perversion and inversion of instinct, who showed the Prussian the way to renunciation of everything but power—power at any price.

Now, considering the Prussian mentality, one may go back a long way beyond Stieber. The Prussian of to-day is clamorously insistent on Nordic purity, freedom from contamination by any anti-Nordic racial intermixture. The insistence is due to an inferiority complex, and to the knowledge that the Prussian is not pure Nordic, if by Nordic he means Scandinavian or of pure Aryan origin.

The reason for this: when Attila's Huns were broken at Chalons, they did not retreat as a single body, but dispersed, and sought food and shelter where they could. One large party retreated so far as the district which subsequently became Prussia: a smaller body, unable to get all they wanted in that area, went farther, and helped to people what is now East Prussia. They raped or otherwise had intercourse with the women of these regions, and so produced the semi-Mongol (semi-Hun) who to-day proudly calls himself a Prussian.

If the mentality, the brutality, and the utter negation of all moral sense, are not enough, then look at the conformation of the skull of the average

Prussian—and see the Mongol declare himself! If one needs an instance, the Prussian of Prussians, son of the Hohenzollern Wilhelm II, provides it. Many portraits of him are available, and every one of them proclaims him more Hun than Aryan. And, if any readers of this work have ever known a Prussian, let them think back and consider the formation of the skull, the high cheek-bones, the nearly slanting eyes, and sometimes the slightly flattened nose, which proclaim descent from the race that Latin genius prevented from over-running the whole of Western Europe.

.   .   .   .   .

The espionage of German diplomacy was, under Hohenzollern rule, regarded as the highest branch of the whole business. Work abroad was done not only by agents specially attached to embassies for that purpose, from servants to military attachés, but even by the ambassadors themselves. A case in point was that of von Holeben, German Ambassador at Washington, who went so far in his efforts at creating bad feeling between Britain and America that public feeling was roused against him in the States to an extent which forced his recall. Bernsdorff, too, went too far, and so far mistook the American temperament that he actually helped in bringing that country into the war on the side of the Allies. So little is the Prussian mentality capable of comprehending the psychological reactions of other races to German efforts.

Which is not to say that those efforts are not dangerous. Diplomatic espionage abroad is very largely a matter of propaganda among the people of the country in which an embassy is situated, and that propaganda is based on the ancient truism to the effect that a lie can be made to rank as truth if it is told well and often. As regards America, and in spite of von Holeben's clumsiness and Bernsdorff's lack of tact, German propaganda had so far influenced public opinion that, in 1914, it was questioned whether the States would or would not enter the war on the side of Germany. An enormous number of agents were controlled and paid from Washington; British oppression of Ireland and misgovernment of the colonies, faked stories of cruelty and even torture, represented Britain as a monster of injustice; atrocities committed by the Senegalese troops employed by the French, and the ruthless injustice of French policy where Germany was concerned—all these and many other perversions of fact were circulated by agents controlled by the German Embassy at Washington. Some of them were so utterly foolish that, in any country nearer the scene of conflict, they would have carried their own refutation, but America, with its fairly high percentage of citizens of German origin, its complex mixture of races not yet fully American in sentiment, was fertile ground for any lie: some could be found to believe and repeat it, and base arguments in favour of Germany on it.

When, as the war proceeded, American opinion swung more and more in favour of the Allies, German effort went beyond propaganda. Instigated and paid by the Embassy at Washington, as was to be proved later, agents began the work of sabotage in munition and other works and achieved some considerable success. There were highly trained and skilled men engaged in this work, some of them so inconspicuously useful that they carried on their activities even after America had entered on the war and the German ambassadorial staff had left the country. And there was, too, under control of the Embassy, a host of *agents provocateurs*, whose business was that of stirring up industrial unrest, with payment by results and almost unlimited funds for expenses. Blunderers of the rank of von Holeben were recalled, and suffered no other punishment. Lesser fry, if their errors rendered them dangerous, or appeared likely to lead to discovery of their associates, were betrayed to the authorities of the country in which they worked. A case in point is that of a man named Graves, who posed as a medical student in Edinburgh not long before the outbreak of war in 1914, and who came under suspicion when an incorrectly addressed letter, containing vaguely incriminating contents, revealed the nature of his activities. As soon as this letter came to the notice of the authorities, Graves was put under observation, shadowed everywhere, and eventually arrested and sentenced to a term of imprisonment. Study of the evidence produced at his trial, especially that of documents produced and read, goes to show that his employers no longer trusted him, and so made the apparent mistake in addressing him which led to detection and arrest.

Since, in the very nature of things, no spy can ever be fully trusted by his employers, the German espionage headquarters instituted a fairly ingenious system of keeping its employees loyal. A certain proportion of the pay was kept back, so that, as length of service increased, a considerable sum was built up and placed to the credit of the spy. Since, in ninety-nine cases out of a hundred, cupidity is the main motive of espionage agents, the system worked very well indeed. No man cared for the idea of forfeiting the nest-egg which would assure his comfort when the work on which he was engaged came to an end.

It has already been noted that, prior to 1914, Germany was allocating upwards of £80,000 annually to espionage work. That sum went to the acquisition of military, naval, and economic information. Diplomatic activities involved the expenditure of further sums, to what extent is not known. The diplomatic agent, moving in exclusive circles, was obviously a very expensive item in the scheme: he had to maintain himself in a way that would place him above suspicion, had to entertain largely, and often to rank as *persona grata* in the highest circles of all. Women, too, were used more in this class of work than in the other grades: in every country considered worth the effort, *salons* existed with hostesses of irreproachable standing, where, in the course of conversation, bits of valuable information leaked out, to be connected up and eventually to reach the Berlin headquarters. In Berlin itself there was, in the good old days, a certain house in great favour among the young men of the various embassies. It was maintained by a very charming hostess whose hospitality was extended to foreigners and young men of her own nationality without discrimination, and the results obtained for secret service headquarters more than justified the outlay.

V

ERNST'S "POST OFFICE"

ONE pleasant summer morning, during the last visit which Kaiser Wilhelm II paid to this country, a highly placed member of the German Imperial Staff went out unattended—that is, he was unattended as far as his own countrymen were concerned: no member of the party moved about London without the knowledge and attention of the police, for visitors of such distinction are always guarded, for their own sakes.

This particular personage headed north-east, and arrived at an establishment kept by one Karl Gustav Ernst, hairdresser, in the Caledonian Road, Islington. Possibly he had a shave, or a hair-cut and shampoo: possibly he had a talk with an old friend who, equal or slightly inferior to him in standing when they had been boys together, had not risen in the social scale as had his visitor. However that may have been, the visit was long enough for more than a mere exchange of courtesies, and then the distinguished caller went back to take his place in the Imperial entourage. And that was that.

Karl Gustav Ernst carried on his peaceful business. It was, or appeared, fairly prosperous: among his clients was an official of Pentonville jail; the local post-office knew him well, for he kept up a fairly extensive correspondence, probably with old clients who had migrated from the Islington district to various parts of England and Wales, and Scotland too. Also, though long established in the Caledonian Road, he kept touch with old friends in Germany, to such an extent that it was thought worth while to investigate the nature of his correspondence, especially that addressed to a person at Potsdam, one named Steinhauer, who sometimes sent bulky missives to the hairdresser.

As a direct result of the investigations, Ernst was arrested simultaneously with Britain's declaration of war on Germany on August 4th, 1914, and charged with contravention of the Official Secrets Act. He denied any knowledge of the charges preferred against him, was remanded, again brought before the court, and recommended for deportation.

This was the initial direct result of the German official's visit to the shop in the Caledonian Road. The indirect results were also achieved on August 4th, 1914: they consisted in the arrests of upwards of nine thousand persons in every walk of life and grade of society; the whole German spy organization in the British Isles was rounded up, and in the Berlin secret service headquarters, instead of the full information of British military and naval movements which had been anticipated, there was blank and utter ignorance as to what was happening in this country. Ernst had been the head "post office" for German agents in Great Britain, and by means of his correspondence they had all been traced in readiness for "the day." Where possible without injury to the British services, they had been allowed to carry on their work for Germany, but every message they sent was carefully checked by the British Intelligence Service before being permitted to go on to Berlin: if it conveyed vital information, either it never went through at all, or else it was replaced by a different, innocuous, or misleading message, carefully simulated to the writing or typing of the sender.

That is not to say that Ernst had been in correspondence with all the spies in the country. Investigation of the correspondence of those to whom he had forwarded instructions and pay from Berlin revealed others, a chain that went on and on until every link of it had been located and marked for action in the event of war.

Confined in Brixton Prison to await deportation, Ernst put through to the Home Secretary an appeal for release from custody. In it he protested his absolute innocence: he was, in fact, a wronged man, against whom the police had been able to produce no evidence, although they had had every opportunity of searching his Caledonian Road premises, where for no less than sixteen years he had carried on an honest and respectable business. Further to that, he was not eligible for deportation, being a naturalized British citizen. It followed that detention of him under the Aliens' Restriction Act was illegal, for which reason he was entitled to demand immediate release.

He got it, only to be arrested as he left the gates of Brixton Prison, on the charge of being a spy in and on the country of which he was a citizen by naturalization. He came up for trial at Bow Street at the end of September 1914, the charge against him being that he "had obtained and communicated, and attempted to obtain and communicate, to one Steinhauer, certain information calculated to be useful to an enemy."

Mr. Archibald Bodkin, who conducted the case for the Crown and was instructed by the Director of Public Prosecutions, made no mention of the

visit which the Kaiser's official had made to
Caledonian Road during the last Imperial visit to
England: even had he done so, it would have been
of no value as evidence. He stated that Ernst had
first come to notice of the authorities three years
prior to the time of the trial, and evidence would be
adduced to show that, from then onward, he had
been a paid spy directly responsible to one Steinhauer of Potsdam, who had been prominent (by
name, that is) in nearly every espionage case that
had come up for trial in Great Britain during the
preceding four years. It had been ascertained that
Steinhauer was an important figure in the German
Secret Service, of which, as evidence would show,
Ernst had been a very active member in this
country.

Steinhauer, Mr. Bodkin stated, had been in the
habit of sending to Ernst letters which appeared to
be ordinary business correspondence, which Ernst
in turn had posted in London to other members of
the German Secret Service. In addition to this,
Ernst's work had consisted in obtaining and forwarding to Steinhauer any information relating to
people in his own district, and any places worth
noting, such as railway stations, depots, and the
like, which might be useful at German headquarters. For these services he had been entitled to
expenses on a fairly liberal scale, and, in addition, a
fixed salary of £1 a month at first, later increased to
£1 10s. a month, "in view of the risk involved in
the work." Probably the main profit was in the
allowance for expenses: a shilling a day, or thereabouts, was small compensation for risk.

From October of 1911 both the hairdressing
establishment and Ernst's mails, incoming and outgoing, were kept under observation. Tracings were

made of all letters addressed to him, before the letters themselves were delivered. He had posted outgoing letters in nearly every part of London to avoid the appearance of constant correspondence between Islington and Potsdam, but, of course, the observation under which he had been kept had rendered his precautions futile. Meanwhile, either from Ernst himself or from other sources, Steinhauer had obtained a good supply of English envelopes and even notepaper, so that Ernst's incoming mail from Potsdam should not be too conspicuous. One batch of these envelopes and paper had certainly been sent over by Ernst himself, marked as "samples" and either understamped by Ernst, or over-weighted when it was examined after he had posted it: however that may have been, Steinhauer had to pay excess postage on it, which clinched his connection with Ernst as fully as if he had signed for a registered package.

But for this matter of excess postage, it might have been difficult to prove the connection between the two, for Steinhauer adopted the pseudonym "Mrs. Reimers" for the purposes of this correspondence. Ernst received letters as "J. Walters," and also as "W. Weller," both names being "c/o K. G. Ernst" at the Caledonian Road address. Enclosed in these sometimes bulky communications were other letters, addressed to various persons at naval ports mainly—Chatham and Sheerness were especially mentioned—and also to centres of military activity. These letters, opened by the authorities, led to some arrests for espionage before the outbreak of war; they helped to bring about the big round-up of August 4th, of which mention has already been made.

Apart from his "post office" usefulness, Ernst

received orders from time to time to inquire into the
lives and occupations of a good many people,
mostly believed by Steinhauer to be connected with
British military or naval intelligence. For these
purposes, Ernst made trips to various parts of the
country; on one occasion he was trailed to Shef-
field, where, evidently, he did a little economic
espionage. He also made contacts with another
German residing at Portland, obviously a naval spy.
Evidence was also adduced to show that Ernst had
posted letters to a man named Parrott, who adopted
the pseudonym "Mrs. Seymour" at a Sheerness
address, prior to his arrest and conviction for
espionage, some two years before the outbreak of
war.

An interesting and very unusual feature of the
case against Ernst was that, after hearing Mr. Bodkin's opening statement, the counsel retained for
the defence announced his decision to withdraw.
He explained this by stating that he had undertaken
the defence in the belief that his client was a British
subject with no designs against the country in
which he had been so long naturalized, and no connection with the enemy. The revelations he had
heard were enough to compel his withdrawal, he
said, and he accordingly threw up the case.

Since the big round-up of Ernst's correspondents
had already taken place, there was no need for the
prosecution to withhold their names, and quite a
number were mentioned in addition to that of the
man Parrott. Among them was that of Graves, to
whom Ernst had forwarded on Steinhauer's behalf
a letter containing £15 in bank notes, which Graves
received at the Central Hotel, Glasgow. Another
was a fireman on H.M.S. *Foxhound*, who had joined
the Navy under the name Ireland, but whose real

name was Kruger: he was nephew of another Kruger who had been arrested and sentenced for espionage work. The German at Portland proved to be one "A. Schutte." Ireland, by the way, had been arrested, but had managed to clear himself and secure an acquittal. Over this, Steinhauer observed in one of his letters to Ernst—"K. (that is, Kruger, Ireland's uncle) has excited himself for nothing. The youth is free. I will relate the story to you orally next time." Which went to show either that Steinhauer made visits to England, or else Ernst took an occasional trip to Potsdam.

There was another letter from Steinhauer, prior to this, and dated January 23rd, 1912, bearing on Ireland's case. It was read in court during the second hearing of the case against Ernst, and said—

"According to information from newspapers, a fireman has been arrested on the English cruiser *Foxhound*. If that is Kr's (Kruger's) nephew, then it is certain that he was dragged into it through the carelessness and stupidity of Kr. Perhaps you can get into communication with K., but by all means be cautious. If my suspicions are correct, then Kr. will be watched. Above all—caution! Should you have opportunity to speak to him, then ask him at the same time respecting a certain Schmidt he once recommended to me. He (Kruger) must be cautious, and especially show no address. That is to say, only go there when you know there is no danger to you. I mean, he must not start speaking German to you in the presence of others. Please let me hear something soon." This letter was sent from Potsdam, and signed "St."

And another from the same source—"Please post the enclosed letters at once and send me, if you please, fifty envelopes as sample which you sent. Then write me a letter, if you please, a letter in good English, in which a customer asks for letters to be forwarded to him on the Continent, addressed to 'Poste Restante, etc.' " The enclosures which Ernst was requested to post were addressed to "F. Ireland," on board H.M.S. *Foxhound* and to "A. Schutte" respectively.

Ernst's reply to this letter was read in court. It had been addressed to "Mrs. Reimers" care of Steinhauer, and was as follows:

"Dear Mr. Steinhauer: Allow me to make a few suggestions which occurred to me while reading the case of Grosse. You will be able to see that your agent Grosse had not the slightest consideration for your other agents. No more could be expected from a man who had already done ten years' penal servitude. Therefore I beg that, when you give any-one my address, you give a different name, such as W. Weller.

"I have immediately posted both letters. Here-with enclosed two sample letters. I should also like to mention that the papers are making a gigantic row respecting the Stewart affair (this concerned a Captain Stewart who had been arrested for espion-age in Germany and sentenced to imprisonment in a German fortress). To-day several papers had the interview and confession which he has made. W. Weller."

The "sample letter," or "letter in good English" for which Steinhauer had asked was also read in court:

"Dear Sir: My business has caused me to go to Switzerland for a short time, and as I shall not be back in London for about two months I should like you to send on my letters, marked Poste Restante.

Any expenses you might incur I will make up on my return to London."

When the fact that Graves had been traced and arrested in consequence of a misdirected letter became known, Ernst sent Steinhauer a newspaper cutting, and observed in a covering letter—"It shows how dangerous it is to have letters addressed Poste Restante. I only say of myself that for £1 a month I will not live in fear, for I have indeed a good business which maintains me. In April I shall end my second year in your service, and I should like to ask that my salary be increased. A confidential post such as mine is worth 30s. a month."

He got his thirty shillings, as already noted. Various other letters, both to and from Steinhauer, were read; the foregoing quotations from the correspondence and statement of the opening of the case are enough to show the working of "post offices" under the system which Stieber inaugurated. Enough, too, to show that the system had not kept pace with the times. The correspondence had been under observation long enough to secure the conviction and sentence eventually accorded to Ernst, before either he or Steinhauer had any suspicion that it was being examined. It was in July of 1912 that Steinhauer first became a trifle uneasy. He wrote, then—"Another point that I wish to impress on you, and that is, always to post registered letters in different post offices or districts. But you do that probably of your own accord." In September he gave another hint of suspicion: "You can imagine for yourself that we need in all directions only good, sure, and trustworthy people. We must be safe from surprises on the part of the women. Will you take another name instead of Walters?"

It may be noted that Ernst had been carrying on business for twelve years and more before he took a hand in the spy game. This was in accordance with the rule laid down by Stieber, and already noted, that agents must establish themselves in businesses in the localities where they would subsequently work, become a part of their surroundings and gain the confidence of their neighbours. Ernst may have been chosen by Steinhauer as a likely person to operate at his post, but more probably he had been assisted in establishing himself there by the German Secret Service, and set to work only when, naturalized and fully settled, he ranked as a good British citizen. In view of the amounts paid to "fixed posts" in French areas, it is more than probable that Ernst relied on his expenses more than on the meagre thirty shillings a month for his remuneration. He was forwarding sums of ten pounds, fifteen pounds, and even more, to various destinations, not—if he were any spy at all—in ignorance of the amounts, and thus held a very responsible position. On occasion, Steinhauer would send him a hundred marks or so for himself: expenses, obviously, but the accounting was a bit loose on both sides. Ernst made his bit.

And Steinhauer was—who? Was it he who paid that call at the Caledonian Road hairdressing shop when the Kaiser last visited England? Beyond question he was an important figure in the foreign espionage department of the German Secret Service, one of the chief spiders at the centre of the web, as the spy trials of the time go to show. The name, like that of the chief of the Gestapo Western Countries organization who sits to-day in Cologne, means nothing, may cover anything. Whatever his real identity may have been, he was obviously cog-

nizant with all military and naval agents in Great
Britain, and acted as paymaster and overseer for
them all, up to the outbreak of war. And, if he were
the one who visited Ernst that summer morning, he
was responsible for the ruin of them all.

VI

FROM THE PRESS: 1914-18

FEELINGS were strong toward the end of 1914, in Britain. In some parts of the country, notably in Kent (first fully organized for V.A.D. work) were Belgians, refugees from Liege, Aerschot, and Louvain. They told stories which, later, were refuted, since the wave of sympathy with Germany which followed on the Versailles Treaty washed out any idea of German brutalities: one had to be kind to a defeated enemy—forget what the Belgians had suffered, if they had ever suffered at all.

A quarter of a century ago those Belgians came to Britain with their stories. I, writer of this book, heard some of them, told by men who spoke broken English, sometimes quite calmly and quietly, sometimes with tears running down their cheeks. One of the calmest and quietest, because he was quite broken-hearted, told how he had been held to watch while Uhlans outraged his wife. . . .

They were denied, all these stories: the rape of Belgium, when our Germanophiles had finished with it, was quite a decent affair: the murders of children at Aerschot—all lies! The sack of Louvain —a regrettable accident, or else it never happened. The concrete gun emplacements round Maubeuge (to move the story from Belgium to France) idiotic fabrications! Things like that could not have happened: the Germans are civilized people; they do not do things of that sort. As for the rape of women and the murder of children—utterly impossible! Your German is a pleasant fellow, a truthful fellow, a humane fellow. And, with a Yankee flavour, Echo says—"Oh, yeah?"

There being quite a few credulous people in 1914, capable of believing the fables told by refugees from Aerschot and Louvain (and especially those who had been lucky enough to escape from Aerschot) toward the end of the autumn the whole country suffered from virulent spy fever. Those who had heard (and been credulous enough to believe) the stories told by impossibly imaginative refugees from Belgium, and from the areas which the Germans occupied in Northern France, got foolishly excited. Where they came across somebody who had German connections, or might possibly be of German descent, or had a cousin whose friend had a nephew who used to write to a German friend, they broke windows, and made rude noises, and generally made life very uncomfortable for the person concerned, though in many cases he or she was entirely innocent of contact with the enemy, and quite a good fellow, really. Spy fever was the fashion, in those bad old days, and, in order to controvert it, the Home Office issued a statement of the counter-espionage measures taken by the British Government. They did not then promise to hang the Kaiser: that was left for a genius of demagogy to issue as his slogan. They told the public the truth as to what had been done, and so made public the existence of what is now known as the "Special Branch" of the Criminal Investigation Department, a body of men quite equal to the Gestapo of to-day in genius, and far superior in cleanliness of method and in decency. Incapable, say, of giving rise to such fables as were told about Aerschot and Louvain, when people were credulous enough to believe . . . the truth.

And here, as told by the Home Office, and published in the Press of that day, is the story of the formation of the Special Branch: although an official statement, it has all the flavour of a good story, and is worth reading as a description of the measures taken against those pleasant workers who had helped to make a land fit for (German) heroes, until the great round-up of August 1914 gave them time to reflect.

"In view of the great anxiety naturally felt by the public with regard to the system of espionage on which Germany has placed so much reliance, and to which attention has been directed by recent reports from the seat of war, it may be well to state briefly the steps which the Home Office, acting on behalf of the Admiralty and War Office, has taken to deal with the matter in this country. The secrecy which it has hitherto been desirable in the public interest to observe on certain points cannot any longer be maintained, owing to the evidence which it is necessary to produce in cases against spies that are now pending.

"It was clearly ascertained five or six years ago that the Germans were making great efforts to establish a system of espionage in this country, and in order to trace and thwart these efforts a Special Intelligence Department was established by the Admiralty and War Office which has ever since acted in the closest co-operation with the Home Office and Metropolitan Police, and the principal provincial police forces. In 1911, by the passing of the Official Secrets Act, 1911, the law with regard to espionage, which had hitherto been confused and defective, was put on a clear basis and extended so as to embrace every possible mode of obtaining and conveying to the enemy information which might be useful in war."

The next section of this statement, without referring to Ernst or to the subject of his activities, states quite clearly his part in the revealment of German machinations in England. As follows:

"The Special Intelligence Department, supported by all the means which could be placed at its disposal by the Home Secretary, was able in three years, from 1912 to 1914, to discover the ramifications of the German Secret Service in England. In spite of enormous efforts and lavish expenditure of money by the enemy, little valuable information passed into their hands. The agents, of whose identity knowledge was obtained by the Special Intelligence Department, were watched and shadowed without in general taking any hostile action or allowing them to know that their movements were watched. When, however, any actual step was taken to convey plans or documents of importance from this country to Germany, the spy was arrested, and in such case evidence sufficient to secure his conviction was usually found in his possession. Proceedings under the Official Secrets Act were taken by the Director of Public Prosecutions, and in six cases sentences were passed varying from eighteen months' to six years' penal servitude. At the same time steps were taken to mark down and keep under observation all the agents known to be engaged in this traffic, so that when any necessity arose the police might lay hands on them at once, and accordingly on August 4th, before the declaration of war, instructions were given by the Home Secretary for the arrest of twenty known spies, and all were arrested. This figure does not cover a large number (upwards of two hundred) who were noted as under suspicion or to be kept under special observation. The great majority of these were interned at or soon after the declaration of war.

"None of the men arrested in pursuance of the orders issued on August 4th has yet been brought to trial, partly because the officers whose evidence would have been required were engaged in urgent duties during the early days of the war, but mainly because the prosecution, by disclosing the means adopted to track out the spies and prove their guilt, would have hampered the Intelligence Department in its further efforts. They were, and still are, held as prisoners under the powers given to the Secretary of State by the Aliens Restriction Act. One of them, however, who established a claim to British nationality, has now been formally charged, and, the reasons for delay no longer existing, it is a matter for consideration whether the same course should now be taken with regard to some of the other known spies.

"Although this action, taken on August 4th, is believed to have broken up the spy organization which had existed before the war, it is still necessary to take the most rigorous measures to prevent the establishment of any fresh organization and to deal with individual spies who might previously have been working in this country outside the organization, or who might be sent here under the guise of neutrals after the declaration of war. In carrying this out, the Home Office and War Office have now the assistance of the Cable Censorship, and also of the Postal Censorship, which, established originally to deal with correspondence with Germany and Austria, has been gradually extended (as the necessary staff has been obtained) so as to cover communications with those neutral countries through which correspondence might readily pass to Germany and Austria. The censorship has been extremely effective in stopping secret communications by cable or letter with the enemy; but, as its existence is necessarily known to them, it has not, except in a few instances, produced materials for the detection of espionage.

"On August 5th the Aliens Restriction Act was passed, and within an hour of its passing an Order in Council was made which gave the Home Office and the police stringent powers to deal with aliens, and especially enemy aliens, who under this Act could be stopped from entering or leaving the United Kingdom, and were prohibited while residing in this country from having in their possession any wireless or signalling apparatus of any kind, or any carrier or homing pigeon. Under this Order all those districts in which the Admiralty or War Office considered it undesirable that enemy aliens should reside have been cleared by the police of all Germans and Austrians, with the exception of a few persons, chiefly women and children, whose character and antecedents are such that the local Chief Constable, in whose discretion the matter is vested by the Order, considered that all ground for suspicion was precluded. At the same time the Post Office, acting under the powers given them by the Wireless Telegraphy Act, dismantled all private wireless stations; and they established a special system of wireless detection by which any station actually used for the transmission of messages from this country could be discovered. The police have co-operated successfully in this matter with the Post Office.

"New and still more stringent powers for dealing

with espionage were given by the Defence of the Realm Act, which was passed by the Home Secretary through the House of Commons and received the Royal Assent on August 8th. Orders in Council have been made, under this Act, which prohibit, in the widest terms, any attempt either on the part of aliens or of British subjects to communicate any information which 'is calculated to be or might be directly or indirectly useful to an enemy'; and any person offending against this prohibition is liable to be tried by court martial and sentenced to penal servitude for life. The effect of these orders is to make espionage a military offence. Power is given both to the police and to the military authorities to arrest without a warrant any person whose behaviour is such as to give rise to suspicion, and any person so arrested by the police would be handed over to the military authorities for trial by court martial. Only in the event of the military authorities holding that there is no *prima facie* case of espionage or any other offence triable by military law is a prisoner handed back to the civil authorities to consider whether he should be charged with failing to register or with any other offence under the Aliens Restriction Act.

"The present position is therefore that espionage has been made by statute a military offence triable by court martial. If tried under the Defence of the Realm Act, the maximum punishment is penal sevitude for life; but if dealt with outside that Act as a war crime the punishment of death can be inflicted.

"At the present moment one case is pending in which a person charged with attempting to convey information to the enemy is now awaiting his trial by court martial, but in no other case has any clear

trace been discovered of any attempt to convey
information to the enemy, and there is good reason
to believe that the spy organization crushed at the
outbreak of war has not been re-established.

"How completely that system had been suppressed in the early days of the war is clear from the
fact—disclosed in a German Army Order—that on
August 21st the German military commanders were
still ignorant of the dispatch and movements of the
British Expeditionary Force, although these had
been known for many days to a large number of
people in this country.

The fact, however, of this initial success does not
prevent the possibility of fresh attempts at espionage being made, and there is no relaxation in the
efforts of the Intelligence Department and of the
police to watch and detect any attempts in this
direction. In carrying out their duties, the military
and police authorities would expect that persons
having information of cases of suspected espionage
would communicate the grounds of the suspicion
to local military authority or to the local police, who
are in direct communication with the Special Intelligence Department, instead of causing unnecessary
public alarm, and possibly giving warning to the
spies by public speeches or letters to the Press. In
cases in which the Director of Public Prosecutions
has appealed to the authors of such letters and
speeches to supply him with the evidence upon
which their statements were founded in order that
he might consider the question of prosecuting the
offender, no evidence of any value has as yet been
forthcoming.

"Among other measures which have been taken
has been the registration, by order of the Secretary
of State, made under the Defence of the Realm Act,

of all persons keeping carrier or homing pigeons. The importation and the carriage by rail of these birds has been prohibited; and, with the valuable assistance of the National Homing Union, a system of registration has been extended to the whole of the United Kingdom, and measures have been taken which it is believed will be effective to prevent the possibility of any birds being kept in this country which would fly to the Continent.

"Another matter which has engaged the closest attention of the police has been the possibility of conspiracies to commit outrage. No trace whatever has been discovered of any such conspiracy, and no outrage of any sort has yet been committed by any alien—not even telegraph wires having been maliciously cut since the beginning of the war. Nevertheless, it has been necessary to bear in mind the possibility that such a secret conspiracy might exist or might be formed among alien enemies resident in this country.

"Accordingly, immediately after the commencement of hostilities, rigorous search was made by the police in the houses of Germans and Austrians, in their clubs, and in all places where they were likely to resort. In a few cases individuals were found who were in possession of a gun or pistol which they had not declared, and in one or two cases there were small collections of ancient firearms, and in such cases the offenders have been prosecuted and punished; but no store of effective arms—still less any bombs or instruments of destruction—have so far been discovered.

"From the beginning any Germans or Austrians who were deemed by the police to be likely to be dangerous were apprehended, handed over to the military authorities, and detained as prisoners of

war; and, as soon as the military authorities desired
it, general action was taken to arrest and hand over
to military custody Germans of military age, subject
to exceptions which have properly been made on
grounds of policy. About 9,000 Germans and
Austrians of military age have so been arrested, and
are held as prisoners of war in detention camps,
and among them are included those who are regarded by the police as likely in any possible event
to take part in any outbreak of disorder or incen-
diarism."

This statement, circulated as widely as possible,
virtually put an end to spy fever: together with such
trials as that of Ernst, to which indirect reference is
made in the course of the statement, it convinced
the average man and woman that the authorities
were wide awake to all possible dangers, and that
the concrete-floored rabbit hutch in Jones's back-
yard was not necessarily constructed as a gun
emplacement.

Before turning to consideration of the final break-
down of the German espionage system as organized
by Stieber, an example of the system's working in a
very important neutral area, the Spanish peninsula,
is well worth a brief survey. That, in various ways,
the German submarine campaign owed a good deal
of its success to depots established on or near the
Spanish coasts, is now as incontestable as that
depots existed on the coasts of Ireland from 1914 to
1918. How Spain itself was influenced by German
propaganda, and how the propagandists fared as
the war went on, may best be told by a series of
quotations from *The Times* of that period. Incidentally, the story thus told gives a good idea of
the sharp division of opinion which existed between the governing and governed classes in Spain,

and which had a definite bearing on the recent civil
war. The quotations are as follows:

1. October 10th, 1914. "The war is regarded as
a conflict between two ideals: the German, represented by the concept of divine right, authority, and
a severe ideal of life and conduct, and the French,
representing that of Socialism and free thought,
tending to corruption and anarchy. These ideas . . .
become strong and articulate in the classes composing what is called Society, and the higher and more
ancient the Society, the more definite they become.
Against this . . . background of prejudice and sentiment there may be discerned a more vital current
of opinion. The whole band of liberal spirits, who
may be described as European in outlook, and who
draw their inspiration from Paris and London
rather than from Rome, are beginning to perceive
that this is a war between freedom and tyranny, and
their sympathies are developing accordingly."

2. February 6th, 1915. "As the evidence of
German intrigue in Spain increases, popular feeling
rises steadily higher. The working-men are protest-
ing in vigorous language against the abuse of
Spanish hospitality, and are expressing the desire
to convey to Germany the hopelessness of the
attempt to induce the nation to take her side in
the conflict."

3. May 3rd, 1915. "The leader of the Reformist
Party, in a speech at Granada yesterday, said he was
convinced that the interests of Spain drew her towards the Allies. . . . In conclusion, a politician
frankly said that he would rather be on the side of a
defeated France and Britain than on that of a victorious Germany. . . . The Liberal organs in particular say that the politician showed with undeniable
logic that Spain can only live if united to France

and England, and by following the fortunes of those
two countries."

4. September 1st, 1915. "*The German Secret
Service*. German agents are busier than ever in
Spain now, propagating announcements of German
victories. Their organization spreads over the
whole country, and even in quite insignificant vil-
lages, where the majority of the labourers cannot
read, individuals in the pay of the German Secret
Service are to be found reading aloud to working-
men from pro-German newspapers which no
Spaniard of the wage-earning class ever dreams of
buying for himself, or even of reading as a gift."

5. September 22nd, 1915. "Such sensational
revelations are being made by Senor Lozano in a
series of articles entitled 'A Liberal Cannot be
Germanophile' now appearing in *El Pais*, that it
was expected the newspaper would be confiscated.
The popular Republican writer states that Liberals of
every shade of opinion are ... united together in their
heartfelt sympathy with the Allies and above all with
France and England. But, says Senor Lozano, and he
brings an overwhelming array of historical facts and
figures in support of his assertion, the Spanish re-
actionaries have never ceased to intrigue with Germany and Austria to restore the Carlist branch of
the Bourbons known to Europe at large as that of
Don Carlos, the Old Pretender, and now that it is
the Kaiser who stands for absolutism all the world
over, the reactionary Spanish Clericals, notwithstanding that the Kaiser is 'the Pope of Lutheranism
and has swept Catholic Belgium with a sea of fire,'
have placed themselves *en masse* on the side of
Germany. William II, in his hatred of Spanish
liberty—the gift to Spain of France and England—
is ready to move heaven and earth to aid the re-

actionaries to bring about civil war in Spain for the third time."

In view of the eventual outbreak of that third civil war, and the side taken by Germany, that fifth quotation is illuminating as regards Spain of to-day. True, there was no William II to further German aims in Spain: there was, instead, a far subtler and more dangerous combination, which used and aided the pro-German elements to produce the results of to-day—for German ends.

6. An article by Lord Northcliffe, September 9th, 1916, contained the following passages: "The Germans have never ceased to agitate for the political and commercial control of Spain. . . . A glance at the map of Europe should be sufficiently suggestive of Bismarck's anxieties about the Iberian peninsula. . . . The Germans in Spain have constituted themselves into a well-drilled army obviously acting on definite instructions. . . . They realize that if to a victorious Germany Spain is very useful, to a defeated Germany Spain is almost essential. . . . The mineral wealth of the Peninsula, only now being scientifically developed, would afford her several sorts of raw materials of which Germany has little or none. And as an outlet for German goods, as the main point of departure for the wealthy Republics of South America, as the bulwark against English control of Gibraltar, Spain is, from the German point of view, distinctly Germany's 'pidgin.'

"The Germans know that, with Spain as a *point d'appui* and with the backing of Spanish opinion and above all with that of the Church, their cause is likely to be better appreciated in the New World than if mother Spain were hostile. From Spain, therefore, proceeds to the New World a great deal of German propaganda in the Spanish language."

7. An article on *Spanish Opinion*, by John Walter. October 5th, 1916. "In every important town in Spain there will usually be found three principal newspapers corresponding to the three chief strata of public opinion: one representing the Church, Carlism, and the forces of reaction, another the Liberal–Conservative upper middle class interest, and another the ideals of the Radical parties. The first, naturally inclined to sympathize with the German cause, made but little difficulty about accepting German patronage and co-operation, and under German protection it grew in violence and resources. The second, true to the official label of 'strict neutrality,' but not without an eye to the prejudices of its readers, fluctuated uneasily between the conflicting opinions and tended to be drawn by the pressure of the surrounding atmosphere into the Germanophile current. The third, as a rule frankly in favour of France and England, as representing kindred political ideas, but receiving neither support nor encouragement from them, was gradually impoverished and undermined by German blackmail and intrigue . . . the strongest sympathizers with the Allies are to be found among the advanced Liberals, Republicans, and Socialists and such-like enemies of constituted authority. . . . Our best friends are to be found among those who are profoundly dissatisfied with the present state of things in Spain. They desire the triumph of England and France as the only chance of a thoroughgoing reform of Spanish life. They dread a German victory as likely to strengthen the forces of reaction and to perpetuate the present political corruption and economic stagnation."

8. By the same writer. December 27th, 1916. "It is a regrettable fact that those newspapers which

enjoy the protection and submit to the censorship of the Church are nearly all passionate and unscrupulous partisans of Germany. . . . The alliance between the reactionary Spanish clergy and the Germans, cemented by the joint control and unscrupulous use of the Catholic press, acts as an effectual muzzle on the free expression of Spanish Catholic opinion with regard to the war."

9. October 3rd, 1917. "As the German cause gradually wanes in the eyes of statesmen and politicians, the Germans are trying desperately to poison the business relations between the great Spanish exporting houses and their English customers . . . and to persuade the fruit-growers and exporters and the hundreds of thousands of wage-earners dependent on them that England is perfidious and selfish, and that Germany is their true friend. In all the chief towns of the south-eastern provinces are to be found little newspapers whose chief function it is to further this strange idea. Some of them are in German hands entirely, while others are directed by priests under high ecclesiastical patronage. All alike traduce England and the English with a unanimity and a persistent animosity which betray a remarkable unity of purpose and control."

10. *The Kaiser's Gifts*, by John Walter. October 5th, 1917. "The active and plausible gentry who operate from the German Embassy in Madrid and from the office in Barcelona soon had it firmly established in the minds of the Spanish clerics that the Kaiser was coming to increase the power of the Church, suppress free thought, and restore the temporal power of the Pope; in the heads of the officers of the Army and the Navy that the German hosts were invincible and that their triumph would inaugurate a golden era of smart uniforms for officers

and discipline for everybody else; and in the minds
of the upper classes generally that the Kaiser's
dearest wish upon the attainment of victory was to
restore Gibraltar to Spain, allow her a free hand in
Portugal, and make her the chief power in Morocco;
that he would put a muzzle on democracy and
inculcate a wholesome respect for authority and a
proper reverence for privilege. These ideas were
busily put about by the Embassy and the Consulates,
and by the thousands of industrious Germans who
were residing in Spain at the time."

11. May 4th, 1918. *Spain's Raw Materials.*
"The Germans here are growing daily more aware
of the vital importance to them of Spain after the
war. She has the minerals and metals which Germany wants for her industries and for her next war,
and also large accumulations of capital only wanting banking and industrial organization to develop
the industries which can serve Germany and dis-
tribute among the Spanish proletariat a stream of
wages wherewith to purchase German manufactured
goods."

12. August 1st, 1918. "Is it in the least realized
how important our interests are here, both now
and after the war?... It is not the Spanish
Government which is to blame; it is our own
Government. Spain gets little help from us, even
that help afforded by a strict regard for our own
interest. There are elements in the situation here
which it would be mischievous to discuss publicly,
but which are present in one's mind as one writes
and add to the gravity with which any well-informed
person must contemplate the tale of the ineptitude
of British policy in Spain since the beginning of the
war. If we do not awake in time, we shall not only
sacrifice infinitely great interests of our own here,

interests which are common to us and Spain, but we may not improbably involve Spain in ruinous calamity and disturb the equipoise of the group of Powers in whose hands the resettlement of half the world will lie. No miracle is required to avoid that catastrophe; only that we should awake and put a little heart and brains into the doing of our work here."

One must discount, in these excerpts, the existence of such prejudices and passions as the war period fostered, and, even so, if for the years 1914–18 were substituted similar dates in 1936–9, the relevance of these passages to that latter period is amazing: history, evidently, is again busily repeating itself. But *The Times* of to-day takes a different view of things, as witness the following article on "Neutral Spain" by its Hendaye correspondent, in the issue of September 7th, 1939:

"General Franco won thanks mainly to the inflexible Crusader spirit which Spaniards fighting under his banner (the old royalist gules and gold) carried in their souls, helped by his superior strategy. . . . Russia was indeed the great enemy of Nationalist Spain. Without her support neither Largo Caballero nor Negrin could have resisted so long. Evidence, piling up since the civil war ended, all points that way.

"After victory General Franco saw to it that the foreign troops which came to Spain should depart. Spain is to be for Spaniards. Help given by Germany has been paid for in great part with ores, grain, and fats. How to ensure that the natural sympathy for those nations who helped in the hour of need shall not interfere with the duties of neutrality is General Franco's problem. The collusion between the author of the anti-Comintern

alliance and Stalin has profoundly altered the outlook of many Spaniards towards Germany. The
bond of gratitude with Italy remains, but in the
absence of any engagement such as was eluded when
Count Ciano came to San Sebastian with it in his
pocket, General Franco's hands are free. The real
difficulties may arise with the incidents brought by
contingencies of war."

How this review of the position can be squared
with the existence in Spain at the present time (late
September 1939) of a total of 1,369 German and
Italian war 'planes, together with their personnel,
is difficult to see. Neither the 'planes nor their
crews are interned: they are merely sitting in Spain,
awaiting orders, possibly with some of that "inflexible Crusader spirit" in their hearts—or fuel
tanks!

VII

COLLAPSE

THE official statement quoted in the preceding chapter, while answering the disturbing questions that were being asked as to what the Government was doing about German espionage, by no means covered the whole field of Special Branch activities. Taken as a whole, these activities were of very great value to the Allied cause: German agents in England had communications with others in France and other countries, and these, with the information gained in the virtual destruction of the organization in Britain, were in some cases altogether wiped out, in others badly crippled.

There remained, however, a very powerful organization in the United States and other neutral countries. So far as most of the neutrals were concerned, action was confined to propaganda and the maintenance of hidden submarine bases: the quality and value of the propaganda is evidenced by the quotations given concerning German efforts in Spain. But the United States was in a different position: long before that country took an active part in the war, it was supplying munitions to Britain and France. Thus, in addition to German propaganda, strenuously circulated by the German Embassy at Washington itself (as was later to be proved) sabotage both in munition factories and in the docks of New York and other ports was a feature of the work carried on, and steadily increased

86

in effectiveness up to the entry of the U.S.A. into the war in 1917.

Prominent among the personnel of the Embassy was Franz von Papen, who, when passports were handed to the Embassy staff, embarked with the rest on the special train provided to convey them from Washington to New York, *en route* for home in diplomatic immunity though, with the entry of the States to the war, they were all kept under close if unobtrusive supervision. On leaving the train, von Papen carelessly—or otherwise—forgot to take with him the private portfolio which he had carefully guarded up to that point, and which was taken by one of the American Government agents on the train, and subsequently examined.

Its contents proved of the utmost importance. They showed that all German espionage in the United States had been controlled by von Papen, and gave illuminating details of the nation-wide activities of the system. In particular the documents found proved that the sabotage in American munition works, especially in and near New York, and the incidents of accomplished or attempted destruction of American ships, had been directly incited or actually carried out by German agents acting under von Papen's orders. It must be understood that, until the portfolio had been discovered and examined, Franz von Papen had occupied a high position in the Embassy, and had been regarded in American circles as an honourable individual—just as much so as the Ambassador himself. Perhaps more so, since Bernstorff had given himself away rather badly by the time he received his passport and went home.

Although von Papen's criminal abuse of his privileges in America would have justified his detention and punishment, he was let go with the rest of the ambassadorial gang. Meanwhile the American authorities communicated details of their discoveries both to Britain and France: the ship in which Bernstorff and his staff had sailed was detained in the Channel while von Papen was closely questioned. In view of the damage he had done, and the atrocious means he had used to do it, there was a question as to whether he were still entitled to diplomatic immunity. He was, however, let go on his way with the rest.

Such documents as he had so strangely left behind gave enough information for the total overthrow of German espionage in the States. In addition to his other responsibilities, he had acted as paymaster, and the funds of the spy system went with him, while the identities of his chief helpers were revealed to the U.S.A. authorities, who took suitable action, and so put an end to sabotage.

A question still to be answered, if ever, is whether the loss of the portfolio were due to carelessness. An astonishing fact is that, although the full circumstances of the catastrophe (from the point of view of the espionage chiefs in Berlin, it was no less) were known even before he arrived in Germany, his career was in no way affected. It is significant that the Ambassador, Bernstorff, faded altogether from public life after his recall, while, at the end of the war, von Papen blossomed out as a very wealthy man.

His close association and personal friendship with Hindenburg is sometimes quoted as accounting for his immunity from the consequences of his "carelessness." It is not generally known that documents existed in the German Chancellory, intimating that von Papen was guilty of something

far beyond carelessness, an accusation which anyone who knew the man with any degree of intimacy
would not hesitate to accept as the real explanation
of what had happened in America. The tools he
had left behind were useless as soon as he had gone,
and therefore he sold them at a price. Such an
explanation is far more credible than that one so
trained in espionage work as was he could have forgotten the portfolio when he got off the train.

Then, long later, the existence of those documents in the German archives came to the know-
lege of members of the National Socialist Party.
Either Goering or Goebbels, probably the latter,
used it to draw von Papen into the series of intrigues
by which the successive democratic Governments
of post-war Germany were destroyed, and by which
finally, his own Chancellorship was transferred to
Hitler. In this, too, is full explanation of his continued adherence to the Nazi party in subordinate
positions, and the nature of the tasks entrusted to
him. Up to the outbreak of the present war, his
allegiance to the party was compulsory, no matter
what was put on him or asked of him. The alternative, a revelation of his treachery and the reward he
obtained for it, would have endangered not only
what position he had, but his life.

Thus, apart from such propaganda activities as
persisted in neutral countries until 1918, the ultimate
collapse of the old German secret service may be
attributed to Franz von Papen. In the immediate
post-war years, the service no longer existed.
Diplomatic and consular authorities had always
been used as integral parts of the machine, but,
after the revelations which came with America's
entry into the war, these ceased to function. Versailles put the finishing touch to the system.

For over seventy years it had functioned, beginning with the internal secret police which Stieber's genius trained and made effective, gradually spreading and increasing in importance, until it covered practically all the world. Materially, it played an important part in the furtherance of the world-domination at which Prussianism aimed. Morally, it exercised a profound influence on the Prussian—if not on the whole German—character. For the whole nation was forced to realize that there existed as part of its life a ruthless, pitiless organization, aiming at the complete subjection of the individual to the State, using any means, and counting baseness equal with nobility for the attainment of its ends. With this as common knowledge, it was inevitable that the national character should be warped: the cynical disregard of truth and utter lack of principle which characterizes German leaders and policy to-day is a direct result of the work of Stieber and his successors.

PART II

NATIONAL SOCIALISM AND THE GESTAPO
Circa 1933–9

I

THE GESTAPO IS FORMED

FOR a period of some twelve years after the signing of the Versailles Treaty, Germany was in a state of political and economic chaos. Each successive Government left behind it a state of confusion worse confounded. The State almost ceased to function as a political entity; social services dwindled, and in some cases altogether disappeared; corruption and immorality steadily increased, especially in the large cities; the debasement and ultimately total bankruptcy of the financial system destroyed the last vestiges of national confidence, and the people were divided into two parts, one of which was apathetic by reason of utter despair, while the other simply did not care—things could get no worse, and there was no prospect of their ever getting better.

There was little or no need, during that period, of external espionage of any kind, and no department which would have taken the responsibility of directing anything of the sort. Throughout those bad years, the intrigues of the various political parties did nothing to restore confidence or stability, until, in 1930, the National Socialist Workers Party (to give it its full title) appealed so greatly to the people that its leaders saw their way to the control of the whole of Germany.

At this point the Prussian mentality, the unchanging force which has so long controlled German destiny, again began to operate, personified in two men who, eventually, were to shackle the German people—this time a Greater Germany—to the principles of Prussianism with its inescapable consequences. Hermann Goering, sometime a member of Richthofen's "flying circus," was direct and forceful, brutally arrogant, a vivid, striking example of Prussianism and everything for which it had always stood: Josef Goebbels, insignificant in stature and appearance, club-footed, crooked physically and mentally—these were the two. Each had ambition to which no limits could be set, and equally limitless vanity: they had nothing else in common, at that time.

Goering had had little to do with politics; Goebbels had tried his luck with every party. The pair of them saw in Adolf Hitler a means to the realization of their common ambition, and so they joined his National Socialist Party, knowing that his policy was based and was dependent for its success on one premise—the complete unification of the German people. Quite surprisingly for such a single-minded and idealistic leader, as he was in those days, Hitler had a very concrete and practical plan of operations, together with a magnetic personality which won him an increasing following.

He enunciated a doctrine, so simple that all could understand it, and resistless in its appeal to the younger generation. It was—"Enlist and unite all German youth for one common ideal, the one which has always appealed to youth with its inchoate longings: purity of soul, the beauty of physical strength, and high adventure for the regeneration of mankind. (German mankind, for a beginning.) If every youth were a Siegfried or a

Galahad, then what limit could be set to their col-
lective achievements? Inevitably, all the women of
Germany would follow this army of splendid
youth, as surely as night follows day. The then
responsible male generation, aimless and despairing
since it had been led, duped, and abandoned in
succession by every self-seeking politician who had
for a time attained to power, could be disregarded.
In effect, let that generation die off: it would in any
case be futile. To consider the case of any single
family, what would be the authority or power of the
father, if he were subjected continuously to the
determined and almost religious conviction of his
sons, daughters, and wife that his political activities,
if any, were inimical to their consecrated duty of
saving Germany—and the rest of the world as well
—by means of National Socialism?"

To the simple mind of Hitler, it appeared that the
youth and women of all the world would follow
along the path blazed by his German youth. He
saw, and possibly still sees, his doctrine as a means
of world conversion: Goering and Goebbels saw in
it a way to world domination, a revival of the old
Prussian ambition: let Hitler carry to its conclusion
the unification and reanimation of the German
people through his "ideals." They, winning influence in the party all the time, were content to
rank as his followers until he had done his part:
then it would be their turn—or the turn of either
one of them who could gain mastery over the other.
Hitler could remain as figurehead. Even by the end
of 1931, his initial aim had been so far realized that
there was no doubt of its swift completion: his
emotional appeals and magnetic attraction had been
supplemented, then, by Goebbels's distorted propaganda, and by Goering's brutal forcefulness

which drew in the military caste to this surprisingly successful movement.

The first great army of youth had by that time been formed, and was represented by some two million brown-shirted lads between eighteen and twenty-two years of age; the younger organization which was comprised of boys between fourteen and eighteen was equally complete. The co-ordinated organizations of girls, young women, wives, and mothers, were already efficient: Germany was in process of being Nazified, and in order to keep it so, and to prevent schisms or cleavages of any kind in the party, the necessity for a secret service of some sort became apparent to the Prussian minds of the movement. Idealism must be backed by secret force: means for intimidaton, suppression, and detection of all adverse influence must be got together. Again the influence exerted on the Prussian character by Stieber becomes evident: clean idealism was not enough: a spy system, permeating all German life and so designed that no man nor family was free of it, must be built up, first to add fear to the other motives binding all young Germany to National Socialism, and then to sweep other nations into the net.

Hitler, visionary and no more, was little interested in this. His magnetism and sincerity had made the two million "Brown Shirts," enthusiastic supporters of the National Socialist movement; they had been organized on semi-military lines and placed under the sole command of a trusted personal friend and comrade, Captain Ernst Roehm. The pick of them had been selected and sworn as Hitler's personal bodyguard, distinguished from the rest by an all-black uniform with silver trimmings. The whole two million had sworn fidelity to Hitler,

and Roehm commanded them only as his nominee.
Hitler's own position in the party, as its leader, was
impregnable: Goering and Goebbels were content
that it should remain so, though they had doubts
from the very beginning about Roehm, and very
soon came to the conclusion that he must be
eliminated.

He was a large, easy-going man, a Prussian run to
seed, with all the virtues and most of the vices of
the old-time Prussian officer. Among other things,
he was a confirmed homo-sexual invert, and it was
not without justice that accusations were later
directed against him of perverting youths of the
Brown Shirt organization. His headquarters
(Hitler's too, until the party came to power and
consequently moved to Berlin) was the "Brown
House" in Munich: there he was to be found
officially, but he had, too, a luxurious villa—using
the term in its Continental sense, and implying
nothing of a merely suburban character—on the
outskirts of Munich. The orgies of which it was
the scene eventually became notorious—justifiably
so.

The planning of a secret police force went on,
and Roehm took for granted that it would be a part
of his Brown Shirt organization—was he not
Hitler's friend? The more live, more active pair
of intriguers saw it differently: they wanted naval
and military intelligence, foreign intelligence, special
branch, and all the rest organized as only Prussian
thoroughness could, independent of everything
else, and controlled by one able, ruthless, single-
minded man. There were thus three men aiming at
control of the projected force: Roehm, complacent
and easy-going, ambitious only within the limits of
his Brown Shirt organization, which he hoped to

persuade Hitler to make the chief military body in
Germany, with himself at its head; Goebbels, master
of words, twisted in mind as in body, to whom the
preferable means of entry anywhere was by the back
door, roof, cellar—any way but that of the front
door; and Goering, who believed that every front
door was made for his use and for that of no other
person.

Time alone would show which of the three would
win, and meanwhile the constitution of the Geheim
Staats Polizei had to be worked out. Since the
party had not yet come to power, the force would
have no constitutional status, but, just as detailed
plans for the instant Nazification of every branch of
the administration of Germany were being prepared, so was it necessary to plan and organize the
skeleton framework of the Gestapo. So far,
Goering and Goebbels had worked together, mainly
because neither trusted the other, and so would not
let him work independently: now, they agreed that
Himmler should be chief of the Gestapo when it
was formed—it was Goering who found and
selected Himmler for the post. With that settled
between them, they had one common object, the
removal of Roehm, left to bind them together.

The formation of the Gestapo and the outlining
of its ostensible functions was left to Goebbels, who
had to submit the completed scheme to Hitler for
approval. In the spring of 1932 all the preliminary
steps had been taken, and, since the constitution of
the Gestapo was completely in accord with the
policy of the Nazi Party, Hitler's approval was a
foregone conclusion. The function of the Gestapo
was that of compelling cohesion in the party, and
consolidating such gains as it made by any and
every means: Hitler, having approved it, dismissed

it from his mind, and it is literally true to say that he, during the next few years, was the only leader of the Nazi Party who did not use or try to use the Gestapo for his own ends.

The actual bringing into existence of the Gestapo could not be undertaken without the active participation of Captain Roehm as "Chief of Staff," and it was for this reason that its functions had been defined to Hitler as a sort of "third estate," extra and supplementary to the work of Hitler himself, and also to Roehm's department. Goebbels made the most of this aspect of the new force to Hitler, and Goering, in quite independent consultations, also stressed it, thus preparing in advance for the demand Goebbels would eventually make, for the appointment of a chief other than Roehm. Meanwhile Roehm, not now so intimate with his friend Hitler as he had been, was left under the impression that he, as Chief of Staff, would automatically take charge of the new department, and consider it a part of his Brown Shirt organization.

Early in 1932 Goering, satisfied with the progress made by the Nazi Party in the Reichstag, and with the chaotic confusion evident in the ranks of the combined political opposition—this latter mainly created by the intrigues of the then Chancellor von Papen—urged Goebbels to proceed at once with the formation of the Gestapo.

If in this recital of events it should be implied that Goering and Goebbels were the only two men in the Nazi Party worth considering, then the implication must be disregarded. At that time, and up to 1934, Adolf Hitler was the only one who counted for anything at all: he had a number of friends, among whom may be mentioned Rudolf Hess, Julius Streicher the Jew baiter, Ernst Roehm, and young

Rolf Zimmermann, this last to Hitler the embodiment of all that was best and noblest in German youth, a very Siegfried—as in fact Hitler renamed him. These personal friends of the Leader had no ambitions that clashed with or rose above his own; there were, too, hundreds of Party leaders of varying rank and influence who had their own hopes of advancement by and through Hitler. Goering and Goebbels, on the other hand, stood alone in that they had seen from the first in Hitler a tool for their own use, rather than a central power under which they too might rise. Others might intrigue within the party: these two saw it from the first as a means to their end, the recrudescence of Prussianism, and used Hitler as their stalking horse.

In March of 1932 a meeting was held in the dining-room of Roehm's apartment in Goethe Platz, Munich; the time was set for ten o'clock in the evening, and the various participants arrived inconspicuously in the quiet, tree-shaded square. There were present at the meeting Captain Ernst Roehm, Chief of Staff; Doctor Josef Goebbels, who had authority from Hitler to constitute the new body which was to be known as the Geheim Staats Polizei; Rudolf Hess, who as Hitler's friend and deputy had always distrusted Goebbels, and was present on his own initiative to hold a watching brief for his friend; Himmler, who was fully aware of the part he was destined to play, but who kept completely in the background; a fifth man, who belonged in Goering's immediate entourage, and who served for Goering as did Hess for Hitler; a sixth, who was of no importance whatever in the internal constitution of the Party, and who was even less German than Hitler himself, but whose presence was nevertheless regarded as indispensable.

The meeting had been arranged by Roehm, who had been advised by Hitler that Goebbels would state the plans formulated for the constitution of the new secret police. This Goebbels did with thoroughness and full detail, showing that not only was the scope of the work to be undertaken by this new force very comprehensive and important, but that the plans had been made with great care and ingenuity. At this meeting, and at one which was also held at Roehm's apartment on the following evening, the constitution of the Gestapo was finally settled, and its activities divided into two parts, one devoted to affairs inside Germany, the other concerned with work outside the country. In both cases it would work in close co-operation with the party machine, which would continue to use the methods of propaganda that had already been found so effective. The technique of the Gestapo, however, would be quite different, though equally efficient.

A remark made at the second meeting illustrates this last point. In answer to a question by Himmler as to where men could be found with the required qualifications for work outside the country, Goebbels replied: "We shall not find them—we shall create them." This was in reference to activities already planned against Czecho-Slovakia, other countries adjoining Germany, together with France, England, and the United States. It was an up-to-date reconstruction of the machine Stieber had constructed, but a far more efficient and deadly thing than his.

In the Central European States, the ground had already been prepared by party organizations formed among the German minorities—as, for instance, that among the Sudeten Germans of

Czecho-Slovakia—and there was no obstacle to the immediate operations of the Gestapo. In the other countries mentioned, considerable preparation was needed; men had to be selected and trained for the work, and it was decided to proceed at once with this, so that, when the National Socialist Party took control of Germany, everything would be in readiness for instant action. Goebbels, at the second of these two meetings, gave it as his opinion that the party would come to power in about a year: the forecast was more than justified when, in February of 1933, Hitler became Chancellor and the Party headquarters at Munich was exchanged for the Government offices in Berlin.

Three things were clearly and finally decided in the discussions that took place over the long dining-table in Roehm's apartment. The first was the constitution of the Gestapo, the second was the emergence of a new technique which was to be applied to the realization of its external aims, and the third that Captain Roehm, in spite of his preconceived ideas on the subject, was not to have control of the force. Throughout both meetings he had been treated by Goebbels and Himmler in particular, and to a slightly less degree by Hess also, with a studied indifference that amounted practically to insult—in his own apartment! His suggestions and opinions had not so much been rejected as ignored, and at the conclusion of the second evening it must have been evident to him not only that there was a movement against him, but that it had grown to an extent which permitted open contempt of him.

Had he been less easy-going, less sure of his own safety through his long association and friendship with Hitler, or had he formed any idea of the implacable hostility of Goering and Goebbels, he would have struck at them both, instantly. Confident in the strength of his Brown Shirt organization, and his own safety in its midst, he remained inactive while the Gestapo, which had been formed with his destruction as one of its primary objects, was put under the control of Himmler.

II

AIMS: INTERNAL AND EXTERNAL

THE aims underlying the formation of the
Gestapo were as simple as its technique was
complex—which is saying a good deal. Internally,
its function was that of consolidating the Nazification of Germany, the actual process of making the
country Nazi being the work of the Party, largely
through its Brown Shirt organization.
In the early stages, the policy of the Party had
been successfully furthered by Hitler's emotional
sincerity, backed by the unstinting and often ruthless support of the Brown Shirts. A point had now
arrived at which a third element was necessary—
intrigue such as the Gestapo could organize and
carry on: Germany was rapidly being made Nazi,
but, when the first enthusiasm for the cause began
to slacken, something had to ensure that the
country was kept Nazi. The formula henceforth
must be: Idealism, backed by Force, maintained
by Intrigue.
The Gestapo was to, and did, penetrate into every
branch of the national life: not only into the private
lives of individuals, but also to the very core of
every institution, whether of the State, political,
economic, industrial, commercial, or financial. It
must penetrate with secrecy and underground
methods, using every means that intrigue could
fashion and supply to ensure that neither institutions nor individuals had secrets of their own—just

as the Party would ensure, by different means, that they had no independent minds of their own.

In Germany itself, this was and still is accomplished by an army of spies, operating in every walk of life and among every class of people: it was and is an adaptation of Stieber's original system, but a tremendously more efficient and complete machine. Brother was set to spy on brother, wives on their husbands; bus conductors listened to and reported on passengers, postmen observed correspondence, friendly strangers in the cafés acted as *agents provocateurs*; school teachers questioned children, while selected children would trap their teachers. Employers must render secret reports on workmen, whilst being themselves subject to espionage by their secretaries, who in turn were being observed by planted office-boys. Men and women everywhere had to walk warily, and give information quickly, lest they should be forestalled and information be given about them.

Here was a combination of the old Venetian system with that of Stieber, elaborated in accordance with the methods of Fascist Italy. Every revolution, too, has produced some such organization, and, although Himmler was not the type that wastes time on the study of history, he had at least studied very thoroughly the methods of the Fascist régime. He was well aware that foreigners visiting Italy were advised by knowledgeable people to refer to Mussolini as "Mr. Smith" if conversing about him, and he was prepared to ensure that in Germany neither foreigner nor native should have even that sort of loophole for criticism of National Socialism or of its leaders.

Other matters formed part of the Gestapo's regular business. There was the "unmasking" of

Jewish international intrigues and financial relations with their co-religionists abroad; there was the discrediting of Communist leaders, apart from the Party drive against Communism as a whole; undermining the position of the military caste, and the destruction of its traditional influence over the army; discrediting all those advisers of the then President of the Reich who were in any way hostile or indifferent to National Socialist aims; using and at the same time discrediting von Papen, then Chancellor; paving the way in the Saar for the forthcoming plebiscite; indirectly using the Brown Shirt organization for all Gestapo aims, and checking the secret activities of individual Party leaders when these were directed to personal ends. Making promises here, lending or withdrawing support there, and double-crossing everywhere.

The principal weapon of the Gestapo was never to be force, for that would be supplied by the Brown Shirts—it would be Fear. Fear planted in the hearts of every man, woman, and child; fear of the sudden loss of possessions and even liberty, of being torn away from home and relatives and friends; fear of the unknown and unexpected, of intimate friends no less than of strangers.

Himmler, the man who was to and did impose this régime on the German people, was well fitted for his task. He was—and is—one who gives the impression of strength, both physically and mentally; he is dark-complexioned, with cold, hard eyes, a tiny black moustache, and lips that seem to but do not smile—the curve that mars their straightness denotes unvarying cynicism, and is the only expression the man ever permits to appear. His judgment is logical, exact, completely impartial, and as objective as it is merciless. No situation would

ever embarrass him or find him unready; whatever
he had to face, he would give it a cold and deliberate
analysis, and deal with each component part in its
proper place, as a separate entity.

He had allowed Goebbels to use his very marked
abilities for his (Goebbels's) own ends, and for that
he was rewarded with his present post; then he
reversed the positions, and used Goebbels to that
Propaganda Minister's undoing.

Immediately after the two meetings at Roehm's
apartment at which the scope and functions of the
Gestapo were defined and decided, Himmler began
to organize and set up his department, though it
would not, of course, be able to operate fully until
the government was in Hitler's hands. This happened only a few months later, and early in 1933
Himmler incorporated in the Geheim Staats Polizei
not only the existing State police departments, but
also all the relevant bureaux of the Ministry of the
Interior and that of Foreign Affairs, and removed
his headquarters from Munich to Berlin. Until
then—that is, while the offices were located in
Munich—Captain Roehm spent most of his time
in Dresden.

Himmler began by selecting the nucleus of his
staff from among the Brown Shirt troops and youth
organizations, and by determining the districts
into which the whole country must be divided for
the purposes of his work. This was done in close
collaboration with the Party machine, which required a similar division of the Reich for its own
redistribution of effective centres when the Decrees,
already prepared, were released to abolish the
separate States of Germany and unify the Reich.
It was finally decided that each Party headquarters,
provincial and district, should have its Gestapo

adjunct, working in close touch with but quite independently of the Party offices.

The existing dossiers of the Police Departments, and the vast mass of documents and evidence found when the Democratic and Communist political parties were liquidated, formed the foundations on which Gestapo activities were built up. At the same time Himmler determined on establishing the nuclei of the headquarters bureaux whose business it would ultimately be to control the foreign activities of the Gestapo. The duties of these offices would naturally be much more complicated than those dealing solely with internal matters, and would require men with different and wider qualifications, but Himmler had no doubt as to his ability to organize them.

Working in close collaboration with his chief organizer for Gestapo activities outside Germany, he decided on Dresden as the control centre for South and South-East Europe, and on Cologne for Western Europe and America. Their geographical positions made these two cities the most suitable. Cologne is the main railway junction which gives immediate access to Holland, Belgium, Switzerland, France, and the western ports, and, due south, connects directly with Austria, Italy, the Adriatic and the North African coast; Dresden has equally direct access to all the roads and railways which run due west and east, from Strasbourg and the Alpine passes to Moscow, Bucharest, Belgrade, Athens, and Stamboul.

Then, since the new technique which the Gestapo was to apply to its foreign activities stressed the importance of economic and industrial penetration, it was thought advisable to form a separate headquarters for the control of military and naval espionage. This was established at Magdeburg, the centre of the civil departments of the Krupp works. All this mass of initial preparatory work kept Himmler and his assistants exceedingly busy during 1932, and everything was ready for instant action when Hitler assumed the Chancellorship early in 1933.

Then Himmler came into his own. His trained staff immediately took up the positions assigned to them, and began to fit into the machine the hosts of young nominees from the Party organizations who had been chosen for training as Gestapo agents. Headquarters were removed to Berlin, the police departments throughout Germany were taken over, the special branches of the Ministry which dealt with all questions of public safety, and the confidential departments of the Foreign Office which were concerned with all secret reports from embassies and consulates abroad, were merged with the secret police, passing under the control of Himmler as its chief.

With all parts of the machine completely in his possession, it remained only for Himmler to fit them together. This he did with all the cold, precise, and thorough objectiveness that characterizes the man; within a very few months the Gestapo had taken root not only in the national, political and economic life of the Reich, but also in the very lives of the people. Between that time and the realization of one of its founders' aims, the elimination of Captain Roehm in the June Purge of 1934, the Gestapo made of itself a force and terror throughout Germany and beyond the southern borders of the country, and Himmler had made his name as widely known as that of Hitler.

This period saw the overthrow of all parties with

aims differing from those of National Socialism. Himmler had the anticipated satisfaction of taking over and using for his own purposes all their records and documents. He played the principal part in breaking Thaelmann, the Communist leader, and personally signed the order for his imprisonment and internment without trial—in the words of the order—"for the preservation of the safety of the Reich." Similar orders were signed for hundreds of other political figures, and for thousands of Jews and others suspected of activities prejudicial to the State—by which was meant the Nazi Party.

An immediate move was made against all the intellectuals whose published work had revealed any tendency to liberalism or liberal sympathies. Some escaped across the frontier, as did Remarque; others, like Ossietzky, did not. Not only the writers, but the publishers who had sponsored their work were sought out by the Gestapo: an instance of this energetic activity was the case of the Berlin agent and publisher of Sinclair Lewis, the well-known American novelist. This publisher just managed to escape to Prague, where he arrived penniless and alone: his wife and family, interned in his stead, served as hostages in the event of his attempting any further activities which might be considered prejudicial to Nazi interests. He was only one of a constant stream of refugees, fleeing from the terror of the Gestapo, that flowed over all the frontiers of Germany, leaving behind them the fruits of their life work, their homes and possessions, and often their families as well. In this latter case, the refugees were still not free of the shadow of Himmler: Gestapo agents were set to watch them, report on and control their activities, the lever used on them being that of their families, still in the power of the Gestapo in Germany. Himmler, with his coldly cynical forethought, had had all this planned in advance.

Preparations had also been made to ensure that the Saar should return to Germany, when the plebiscite of January 1935 was held. The territory, as it then was, lent itself admirably to Himmler's methods. The régime of the High Commissioner, appointed as governor of the Saar by the League of Nations, was artificial, unsuited to the realities of the position, which, in fact, the League and its nominees never fully faced—perhaps never fully realized. Such few attempts at the preservation of order by foreign police as were made failed—inevitably: the tiny territory was overrun by hordes of refugees from Germany proper, by Jews, Communists, well-meaning but ineffectual intellectuals, and opportunists of all kinds. The French and German parts of the administration were constantly at loggerheads; French commercial interests were grasping and intolerant, with the German side, directed by the Gestapo, out to make the most of every incident; the High Commissioner had no real knowledge of what was going on under the surface of things.

No ground could have been better prepared than was this for the horde of agents that Himmler turned loose upon it, nor is it surprising that the Saar returned to Germany, so effective was their work, with a 96 per cent preponderance of votes. Party methods were sufficient to influence the purely German part of the population, in conjunction with their dislike and distrust of the French. The Gestapo dealt with the refugees, who were numerous enough seriously to have affected the results of the voting—dealt with them in the usual way. Every refugee was individually investigated, hounded, and threatened, and in every case in which a relative of the person concerned could be traced within the borders of Germany proper, that relative was arrested and interned as a hostage for obedience to Gestapo orders. Those over whom no such hold could be obtained were systematically terrorized, even beaten up, and all who were regarded as dangerous from the fact that they showed qualities of leadership or organizing ability received special attention, often being removed, forcibly and secretly, across the border and back into Germany. Thus, yet again, did Himmler justify his appointment as Chief of the Secret Police.

Apart from these routine activities of the Gestapo, Himmler found time to take part in the internal intrigues of the Party itself. Over the affair of the Reichstag fire, he threw in his lot definitely and finally with Goering, and helped that astute Prussian to place the first stumbling block in Goebbels's path. The burning of the Reichstag had been definitely engineered by Goebbels himself, with the active consent and assistance of Goering. The actual operations had been carried out so openly that Goering and Goebbels were known to have been inside the building less than an hour before the fire was discovered. This apparent disregard of consequences was due to Goebbels's belief that all the necessary evidence for showing that the fire was the work of Communists had been provided by Himmler, who would produce it when required.

Most unfortunately, from the point of view of the Minister of Propaganda, Goering had arranged with Himmler that this faked "evidence" should be suppressed, and that the task of fixing on the Communist Party the responsibility for the outrage should be left to Goebbels's unaided powers of invention. That he was unequal to this unexpected call on his ingenuity became evident as the months that followed brought inquiry after inquiry, which the discomfited Minister was utterly unable to satisfy; the execution of the semi-cretinous, wandering Dutch youth—who was not even a Communist—failed to clear Goebbels of suspicion, and it was from this point that his influence in the Party began to decline, while that of Goering correspondingly advanced.

It must be realized that Hitler knew nothing or next to nothing of these undercurrents; he would have been very grateful to Goebbels if that worthy could have produced clear evidence that the Communist Party had destroyed the Reichstag, for he would then have had just cause for immediate and finally effective action against the Communists. As it turned out—or rather, as Goering made it turn out—Hitler had no cause at all to be grateful to his Propaganda Minister, in view of the embarrassment that resulted.

Thus, from its foundation, the Gestapo played its sinister part in the internal affairs of the Reich; meanwhile, the branch of its organization destined for operations outside the borders of Germany was rapidly taking shape. The external activities can only be realized to the full in conjunction with the aims of the Nazi Party as a whole; on these latter, Gestapo work outside Germany was and is based, and on that work the furtherance of Nazi policy throughout the world is largely, if not mainly dependent: the two must therefore be outlined together.

.   .   .   .   .   .

When the Gestapo was first formed, the world policy of the Nazi Party had not been fully determined: it existed only in broad outline, but to an extent that showed how far-sighted were the Party plans: it went far beyond the limits defined in *Mein Kampf*, and declared how Hitler's ideal of world domination was being interpreted by Goering and Goebbels, representative as these two were of the revival of Prussianism.

The plan, ultimate expression as it is of Prussian aims, is in effect world-domination at all costs; the Nazi Party as dominated by Goering had and has no doubt that it will be finally achieved. Its first step was to be a modification of the "drang nach osten" as given in *Mein Kampf*. Here it must be realized that Hitler's campaign against Communism in general and Soviet Russia in particular, with its provision of "lebensraum" for the German people in the Ukraine, was not even in 1932 accepted by Goering, whose plan was much more far-flung. Goering saw that the neutrality of Russia was essential to the success of his more comprehensive aims; saw, too, even at that stage, that it would be easy to make sure of Russian neutrality, when the need arose.

Hitler's emotional campaign, therefore, was directed towards the Ukrainian minority of eight millions in Poland and in the province of Ruthenia, not with the idea of opening a way for the penetration of Russian Ukraine, but to begin the disintegration of Poland and Czecho-Slovakia. What may be termed the complete initial objective of the party plan was control of the Mediterranean, to secure which a number of steps had to be taken in succession.

As a beginning, Austria had to be acquired to

establish contact with Italy; then control of South-eastern Europe and the Balkans must be assured; political dominance in Spain came next, and, after that, the break-up of all French alliances in Europe, and the reduction of France by these means, and by deliberately fomented internal dissensions, to the status of a second-class Power; with this would come about the isolation of England—so it was foreseen.

Following on all this, the disintegration and final acquisition of all the French North African colonies was to be achieved; then the subjugation, by force, if necessary, of Egypt and the East African coast in preparation for the move against British South Africa, which would put the whole African con-tinent under Nazi domination. Japan was to be encouraged to acquire mastery in the Far East, and at the proper time to have so far gained control that British influence and interests east of Singapore would have ceased to exist. Japan would also be permitted, and even encouraged, to occupy Austra-lia: the need for "lebensraum" in Japan was and is as urgent as that of Germany (far more urgent, in fact) and China with its already dense population offers no outlet. For the crowded millions of Japan, as Nazi Germany sees it, there are but two alterna-tives, "lebensraum" or birth-control, and the only available "lebensraum" is the undeveloped con-tinent of Australia.

The revolt of India was also taken in as part of the plan, and Nazi Germany, at the proper time, would assist in making the revolt successful. Then, as regards the Western world, Japan had a further role to play: she was to act as a constant menace to the United States, and thus keep American eyes fixed on the Pacific—Australia was the bribe for this piece of work. It was decided in Nazi minds that,

for her own salvation, Canada would throw in her
lot with the States, since England would be unable
to aid her in guarding her western seaboard. Thus
with no interests left in Europe, cut off from the
Empire that had once been, and with the United
States far too occupied with its own troubles to lend
a hand, England would be completely isolated—no
more than a grey little island with no power to influence European affairs, let alone those of the rest
of the world. "Deutschland (Nazified) uber alles!"

This, summarized to the barest essentials, was the
plan which formed in Goering's mind and gained
coherence as the party came to power. Hitler fully
concurred in it, but Goering presented the plan to
him in such form that he was fully convinced it
could be achieved without war. Uni-lingual, simple
man of the people that he is, Hitler came to power
with much to learn: his Prussian masters took good
care that he never learned it: Goering had no delu-
sions as to the inevitability of war before all that he
and his like planned had become realities.

This brief excursion into the political aims of the
party is necessary for understanding of the Gestapo
organization for work outside Germany, formed
solely for the furtherance of party ends. At the
time of its formation, the Gestapo had for its immediate external aims the complete disintegration
of Austria, and then that of Czecho-Slovakia, as
preliminaries to annexation of both States by the
Reich. Next came preparation of the way in
Poland for the re-drawing of German frontiers in
the East. Next, effective measures must be taken in
Roumania to ensure the return of the Dobrudja to
Bulgaria, Transylvania to Hungary, and possibly
(only if absolutely necessary as a bribe) Bessarabia
to Russia. Then came the need for assurance of the

complete economic dependence of Bulgaria on the Reich: the internal disintegration of Jugoslavia, to prepare for the complete political dominance of Germany and Italy, or a possible territorial division; measures to secure the political and economic adherence of Turkey and Greece to the Reich; effective political intervention in Spain; political and economic sabotage in France; economic espionage and intrigue in England; economic and political penetration in South America; espionage and economic and political sabotage in their widest forms in the United States, fertile field for propaganda of any sort.

This may appear too ambitious a programme, and one beyond the powers of any one man, or even of any one organization. But so much can be proved to have been done as to show that the whole may yet be possible.

III

EXIT ROEHM

IN the period now under consideration, 1933-4, Goering and Goebbels, next to Hitler himself and in order of their respective places, led the Nazi Party. They had with them von Papen, using his undoubted powers of duplicity and intrigue for the furtherance of Nazi aims, and they had the strength of Hitler's personal magnetism on which to rely if difficulties should arise. A sentence of Goering's— "If anything should go wrong, we can always get Adolf to weep," is evidence of his real opinion of their Fuehrer. Von Ribbentrop had not yet come to prominence: these two figures occupied the back centre of the stage, with Hitler in front, promising virtually heaven upon earth to a Nazified Germany —or, more accurately, all the kingdoms of the earth.

They had to get rid of Captain Ernst Roehm, Chief of Staff, and thus head of all the party forces —with the exception of the newly-formed Gestapo. As they knew, he had already asked Hitler for the rank of General, and wanted his Brown Shirts to become a permanent organization. The influence he wielded, and they feared, may be gauged from the fact that he was included as Reichsminister in Hitler's first Cabinet, a post which confirmed him in his control of internal affairs, backed as he was by his two million Brown Shirts.

Goering, determined on making himself head of

the Reichswehr and master of Prussia, looked round
and saw that there were a few generals of the
military caste who must be eliminated, in addition
to Roehm, because they would never accept a mere
captain such as was Goering himself, a swash-
buckler already running to fat (in their view) with
his overbearing ways and insensate ambition, as
their superior. Goering marked them all down for
destruction—when he should have no more use for
them. Roehm had to be destroyed too, because of
his military aspirations, which clashed with Goering's own.

Goebbels, for his part, saw Roehm as one whose
influence on Hitler was incompatible with his own
advancement. It was through him, though by
Goering's initial instigation, that Himmler instead
of Roehm had been made chief of the Gestapo.
The new force, in no way affecting Roehm's personal friendship with Hitler, deprived him of a
large part of his power, and now Goebbels opened
his campaign for the complete destruction of
Roehm. This took the form of propaganda in the
party, together with insidious hints to Hitler, to the
effect that, throughout the whole of the Brown
Shirt organization, corruption, immorality, and
especially homo-sexual practices were on the increase, and that it was necessary, at this critical
time of the Nazi assumption of full power over
the State, that a standard of purity in conduct,
equal to the purity of Hitler's own aims, should be
maintained.

Bearing in mind the closeness of Hitler's friendship with Roehm in the very early days of the
party's formation, it is scarcely conceivable that he
was altogether ignorant of the things at which
Goebbels so insistently hinted. All Germany had

been corrupt and immoral; Roehm was but one among many. It is probable that, at the very beginning of their acquaintance, the ex-house-painter looked up to and admired his friend with the military bearing and ease of manner, so different from his own emotional fervour and—at that time—unrealized ambitions. When he gave this friend control of the Brown Shirt youth, he must have known what opportunities he was offering; perhaps he considered his own influence for clean living and idealism as irresistible, and enough to nullify Roehm's temptations to Brown Shirted youth. But now Goebbels whispered, hinted, with a view to Roehm's downfall.

Goering did his bit, pointing out that the immorality prevalent among the Brown Shirts was antagonizing the Reichswehr, and, of course, with the Reichswehr the whole of the powerful military caste. Between them these two played on Hitler's mind as on a delicate instrument: it took them a long time to accomplish their purpose to the full, because Roehm was Hitler's friend, while they were, unknown to him, merely his masters. Because their task was so difficult, they had to go farther than they had first intended, to achieve it fully. The complete party purge was incidental to the elimination of the men marked by these two for destruction.

Goering brought in on his side, through von Papen, the army generals he intended to remove, on the pretext that both they and the Reichswehr would be dominated by Roehm, if the Brown Shirt organization were given military status. Goebbels enlisted all those party chiefs whose ambitions were blocked by the dominating position of the Chief of Staff. Both enlisted the aid of Himmler,

who double-crossed the pair of them until he
had worked out the exact position he wanted to
occupy, and finally threw in his lot with Goering.

By 1933, when all Hitler's entourage was moved
to Berlin to form the first National Socialist
Government, the machinations of these two had so
far advanced as to leave Roehm, a Reichsminister,
behind in Munich, separated by all Germany from
Hitler, his leader and friend. The fat, easy-going
Chief of Staff saw no particular danger in this
arrangement: in any case, neither ambition nor
possible duties in Berlin would have dragged him
away from the headquarters of his Brown Shirts in
Munich. He knew, too that his position as sole
head of all the semi-military organizations of the
party rendered him unassailable except by Hitler
himself, who was not only his party chief, but also
his personal friend.

The task undertaken by Goering and Goebbels
was, therefore, no light one. Perhaps they would
never have succeeded in it, but for one circumstance
which must be fully realized, difficult though it may
be of explanation.

To Hitler's simple and direct mind, his sudden
accession to supreme power meant that his dreams
were realized, and that, now, he could yield himself
completely to the visions which comprehended his
ideal of world-domination. His detachment and
mysticism increased; he became in his own mind
the Reichsfuehrer, which meant, to him, the spiri-
tual leader of the German people: he was, now,
the very torch itself which his army of German
youth should bear throughout the world. This
development of his mentality had undoubtedly
been foreseen both by Goering and Goebbels,
and the moment of its arrival was beyond question

that in which they should put their plans into operation.

It was unfortunate for the pair that everything should hinge on a personal friend of Hitler: neither of them desired anything approaching a party purge, but so many currents had been set moving in this relentless campaign to force Hitler to destroy his friend, that something in the nature of a purge was now inevitable.

That the outside world might regard it as a sign of weakness, and an indication that the revolution was beginning to feed upon itself, was unfortunate, but could not be avoided. The two arch-conspirators hastened to adapt all possible contingencies to their own advantage.

Goebbels made swift overtures to the still powerful party leaders in Bavaria and Saxony, and to members of Roehm's staff, his idea being to gain control of the Brown Shirt organizations, and thus automatically to defeat Goering's aims. Goering moved equally swiftly—or, to be exact, von Papen did so on his behalf. The military bloc joined him in final urgent representations to Hitler, extending the accusations of corruption, immorality, and all the rest of it, to the whole Roehm administration, and expressing grave fears for the safety of the youth organizations, and for the loyalty of the Reichswehr.

The price offered to the generals for their support in this was the military governorships of all the provinces; these same governorships, but in civil rather than in military form, had already been offered to the provincial party leaders by Goebbels to ensure their support. It was a situation which could have only one outcome: the man who won would be the master of Germany.

At last Hitler moved, and consented to Roehm's

removal, but, a full week after his capitulation to
Goering, he had still taken no steps to give effect to
his decision. Until he did so, Roehm, in the centre
of his Brown Shirt stronghold at Munich, Chief of
Staff, and thus under Hitler in control of two
million armed men, held a position so far removed
from the control of any other department of state
that he could consider himself quite safe. Had he
not been Hitler's trusted friend, he would never
have attained to such a position of complete
immunity.

Goering, impatient at the delay, played his last
card. He induced Himmler, chief of the Gestapo,
to inform Hitler that a widespread plot for the disruption of the party had been discovered. It was
backed by General von Schleicher and the military
bloc, who were certain of their ability to control
and direct the Reichswehr. It had the support of
Roehm, who intended to use the Brown Shirt
organization to seize all the provincial governments.
Both von Papen and Hugenberg, the great newspaper owner, supported the plot, Himmler said, but
von Papen had withdrawn and passed the information to the Gestapo.

On receipt of this information Hitler hurried to
the one spot which he could regard as sanctuary,
the apartment of Joachim von Ribbentrop, which
he had used since early in 1933 as a meeting-place
for secret interviews with the then Chancellor, von
Papen, and other political leaders. There, in an
emotional scene, he entrusted to Goering the task
of suppressing all disaffection. All, that is, with the
one exception of Captain Roehm: Hitler himself
would avenge this betrayal of his friendship—this
cynical betrayal of all his ideals, this obscene
betrayal of German youth! No other should be

allowed to take any part. There was no moving Hitler from his purpose: he would go to Munich alone.

This, of course, was for Goering an entirely un-foreseen complication. It left Goebbels, the doctor of words, at a loss, but provided an opportunity that Goering, the man of action, instantly seized. He swiftly outlined a plan which provided for him to go first to Munich, arriving quietly in the early evening: he would take immediate steps to isolate Roehm, and confine the Brown Shirts to their quarters, using if necessary Hitler's name as his authority. He would then at once return to Berlin to attend to matters there, and late the same night, Hitler could fly to Munich and find all the pre-liminary work accomplished. In this, it must be understood, Goering's main aim was that of pre-venting any reasonable discussion between Hitler and Roehm. He knew that, if he could provide for Hitler's arrival in the small hours, at Roehm's villa rather than at the Brown Shirt headquarters, Roehm would be found either in the midst of an orgy of dissipation, or in circumstances still more compromising. To the intense chagrin of Goeb-bels, Hitler agreed to the whole of Goering's plan. Thus the stage was set for the night of the June purge.

·   ·   ·   ·   ·

The only authoritative account of the events of the June purge is the official statement issued by Goebbels, who acted on instructions from Hitler and Goering. It is wholly inaccurate: obviously it could not be otherwise. So many conflicting interests had seized the opportunity of settling personal grudges, or clearing the way to individual advancement, quite apart from the main issues involved, that no one man in all Germany had any clear idea of the whole. It is known, however, that at least 1,400 people were killed, and not less than 7,000 were removed to concentration camps. For the greater part of the killings, the responsibility rests with Josef Goebbels.

It was Goebbels who spread the disaffection among the provincial leaders, and held out hopes of great reward to the more ambitious members of Roehm's staff. It was this section, working largely in the dark and with no coherent knowledge of the whole plot, which both suffered and caused the greatest slaughter. It is also certain that Goebbels himself contrived the deaths of a number of provincial leaders and propagandists in the south-east and in Saxony, amongst them being the former Prime Minister of Bavaria.

Goering's part was as direct and brutal as his mentality. Apart from the removal of Roehm, he intended to destroy every member of the military caste who might prove a danger to his ambitions. He did so, ruthlessly and efficiently. Immediately on his return to Berlin, his pre-arranged plans were carried out. His guard hurried to the residence of General von Schleicher, the former Chancellor, who not only stood in the way of Goering's military aspirations, but who could also stand as a barrier between Goering and his intent to seize all internal power in Prussia. It is still significant that, in spite of all Hitler's decrees unifying the Reich and abolishing provincial governments, Goering has blandly declined to relinquish his premiership of Prussia.

At von Schleicher's house, the general was killed in cold blood, and in utter ignorance of any reason for the outrage, after his wife had first been shot as she tried to protect him. His secretary and servants were arrested and hurried to a concentration camp within a few hours. Simultaneously seven other generals of the Reichswehr, who with von Schleicher formed the military *bloc* opposing Goering, were sought out and killed. This was the extent of Goering's participation in the "Purge."

Hitler himself dealt with Ernst Roehm, his friend, and to what happened there were only four eye-witnesses, no single one of whom has spoken until now. All the other deaths were incidental to these ten, and, of the ten, that of von Schleicher's wife was not planned. The hundreds of killings due to Josef Goebbels were the result of his tortuous intrigues and helped only a few obscure men: they helped Goebbels not at all. The nine deaths due to Hermann Goering helped nobody but Hermann Goering himself, and him they helped a lot. The one death due to both Goering and Goebbels, that of Captain Roehm, made Goering master of Germany and Goebbels a nonentity. Made finally of Adolf Hitler a tragic figurehead, settled for all time the meaning of world domination in the Fuehrer's dreams, saw the final triumph of Prussian mentality, opened the road to Godesberg and Munich, and rendered inevitable the declaration of the British Government on September 3rd, 1939.

. . . . .

In the late afternoon of June 20th, 1934, the Prime Minister of Prussia arrived in Munich alone and unheralded. He learned that Captain Roehm and his immediate entourage were at his villa on the Munich–Weissensee road. Proceeding to the Brown House, he entered Roehm's secretariat alone and unannounced, and took complete charge, in Roehm's absence, in the name of the Fuehrer. He sent immediate orders to all gauleiters that all guards were to be withdrawn at once from duty and confined to their quarters and barracks. All telephone lines were rendered ineffective. He forbade any guard or party member, whatever his rank, to leave the Brown House until further orders. He ordered four Mercedes cars, manned by twenty Black Guards of Hitler's own escort, to stand by in the inner courtyard of the Brown House. In the private office of the secretariat, he went hurriedly through Roehm's files, destroyed a number of documents, and left in their place certain other papers which had been supplied by Himmler.

He spent fifteen minutes alone with a blond youth who had arrived with him on the train from Berlin, and he then flitted away from Munich as unostentatiously as he had come there. The blond youth, Rolf Zimmermann, was Hitler's personal liaison officer, and one of the eye-witnesses of that night's work.

In all the swift, smooth progress of Goering's work there had been only one disconcerting incident: he had come face to face with Goebbels in the huge foyer of the Brown House: Goebbels was also unattended and alone, and for possibly the first time in all his career he betrayed a momentary embarrassment. Goering, massive and domineering, informed his rival that he, Goering, alone had power to act in Munich, and Goebbels immediately left. Where he went and what he did are things known only to himself: anyone with any knowledge of Josef Goebbels will know that, whatever account he might give of his actions of that night, it will be far removed from the truth.

The old-world cobbled streets of Munich looked oddly deserted on that summer evening without the usual throngs of brown-uniformed guards and the long lines of luxurious party cars. There was a curious feeling of apprehension, a shadow as of events to come. About midnight, the four big, black Mercedes cars left the Brown House. The first of them was Hitler's own car: it held only the driver and two Black Guards. The remaining three were packed with eighteen guards, and in addition the second car held Zimmerman, the blond youth who had spoken with Goering, and one other man who wore neither uniform nor party badge. The line of cars was almost invisible, their blackness and that of the uniforms blending into the darkness of the summer night. There was only an occasional gleam of silver buttons and buckles.

The cars proceeded rapidly to a quiet entrance of the air-field and drew up in deep shadow. Nobody got out, and only the occasional flash of a petrol lighter as a cigarette was lighted betrayed their presence. Some time before the dawn came the drone of a powerful aeroplane: far out on the landing-ground lights directed the descent and landing of the machine, and there was shadowy activity about if for a while. Then a single figure, wearing a belted raincoat, emerged hurriedly from the gloom and entered the first of the four cars.

The four immediately set off and, travelling at high speed, took the Weissensee road. Some miles from Munich they stopped again, near the white-painted gate of a large villa standing on the left of the road. No words of command were heard: the night was dark and very still. Then came a scuffle of heavy boots on the sanded roadway, a low-toned,

harsh—"Achtung! Der Fuehrer!" and the solitary
figure of a guard just beyond the heavy gateway
froze into immobility. There was an impression of
a host of shadows, deeper than the normal shadows
of the night, converging on the front of the villa,
from which no light showed. The crash of an
opening door sounded startlingly loud, and an
electric bell shrilled clangingly from within the
house. There was no sound of footsteps on the
thick rugs and carpeted stairs. Suddenly a few
lights flickered here and there, dispelling only a
little of the gloom in the vast rooms and wide
corridors of the villa. From an open door on the
left of the hall came the glitter of silver and glass on
a long, polished dining-table, and a glimpse of a
sleeping man lolling grotesquely in a chair. Then
the shocking sound of shots, and the smell of
blood: there was practically no other sound: only a
few hushed murmurs.

At the head of the first flight of stairs were three
doors. On the threshold of one stood the two
Black Guards who had been in Hitler's car. Inside
the room, between the bed and the window, stood
Adolf Hitler, with an emptied automatic pistol in
his hand. To one side stood the blond youth, and
the man who had been with him in the second car.
On the far side of the bed lay the naked body of a
youth, who had been shot repeatedly in the face
and breast, and all the whiteness of the bed had been
changed to a crimson blotch, while one of the
Black Guards, standing by the door, held in his
hand an automatic pistol which still smoked.

Beside the body of the youth lay that of Captain
Roehm, one arm outflung so that the fingers trailed
on the floor from the low bed. The bedclothes had
been stripped down and tossed over the rail at the

foot: Roehm's face was unmarked, but all his left breast was a bloody laceration where the shots had plunged in and through. Little streams of blood had run down the outflung arm and begun to form pools on the gaudily coloured carpet: the body had shrunk, apparently, gone flaccid, and now in death the face appeared singularly calm. The body of the youth at his side lay as if still asleep, despite the fact that the face was almost destroyed.

For the space of many seconds there was complete silence and immobility on the part of the five living people in that room. No one of the four others looked at Adolf Hitler's face. Thin wisps of grey smoke floated through the open doorway. The sound of shots about the rest of the house had ceased, and hurrying footfalls, muffled almost to silence by the thick carpeting, sounded on the stairs. Abruptly Hitler stalked past the two guards without a word, and went down the stairs: the other four in the room followed him.

The other doorways on this upper landing were opened, and on the thresholds, as if they had been taken from the beds and thrown with violence, lay the naked bodies of youths. The open door of the dining-room in the lower hall still revealed the seated figure, but now it drooped more grotesquely, a corpse.

There was no more silence, but the high-powered cars roared back along the road to Munich. A few hours later, the Reichsfuehrer was in Berlin: with him had gone the blond youth who had seen it all —Rolf Zimmerman.

Thus by intrigue, by cynical betrayal, by cold-blooded treachery, and by murder, two of the aims for which the Gestapo was created had been achieved. Two men, in their insensate craving for

power, had fashioned this machine: among the
objects of its use, one had been the elimination of
Roehm, and another that of setting the feet of the
German people irrevocably on the road to world-
domination by force. Both were now accomplished.

IV

SABOTAGE OF A REPUBLIC

DIRECTLY after the formation of the Gestapo, its external activities were turned toward Czecho-Slovakia, with objects clearly defined, and the means by which they were to be realized mustered and directed by the men whom Himmler had chosen. The list of objectives was a formidable one; it consisted of a whole series of operations, the cumulative effect of which would be that of removing—or rather, of rendering it possible for Germany to remove—Czecho-Slovakia from the map of Europe. Work to this end was begun as early as 1933.

The programme may be described as one of dishonourable ruthlessness. By influence brought to bear on German, Slovak, Hungarian, and other minorities in the military establishment, disaffection was to be created in the army to such an extent that mobilization on a war footing would be impossible; the Central Government was to be undermined and rendered ineffective, also by the use of these minorities; municipal and provincial administrations were to be corrupted by means of bribes and threats, and the racial minorities of the State were to be so worked on by Gestapo agents that they would refuse to co-operate with any form of Czech control, and would threaten open revolt.

Further, and for the benefit of any possible allies of the Republic, evidence had to be manufactured, since it did not exist, to show that the Czech Government was lending active support to Communist elements, and intriguing with the Soviets against the interests of the Reich; that Czech industry was engaging in operations, in conjunction with foreign countries, that threatened the economic security of the Reich; Czech youths, wherever possible, were to be stirred to discontent, and to suspicion of political and social conditions; saboteurs were to be introduced into all the principal industries, to bring about complete industrial paralysis throughout the country when—or if—necessary; military fortifications were to be mapped and their effectiveness nullified, and, finally, the German minority of the Sudeten areas was to be effectively armed.

The Nazi Party itself, already firmly established in Czecho-Slovakia, could undertake some part of this work, but the intimate and important part called for the technique of the Gestapo rather than for the normal party propaganda methods. These latter were to be directed to the sabotage and internal disruption of the democratic political parties throughout the country.

Formidable though it appeared, the whole programme was completed to its last detail by the Spring of 1937. Then, with Austria fallen, the heritage of the Hapsburgs completed the geographical outline of Germany in the south-west, and Hitler knew that Czecho-Slovakia was his to take; Goering knew that the road to the south-east was open, and that Jugoslavia, Roumania, and the Balkans generally comprised no longer a threat, but an asset; Hungary was already more or less secretly a co-partner, with Horthy holding the fort in Hitler's interests, while in Russia Stalin would help rather than hinder. The hypocritical policy of Italy was decided, the role of Spain was fixed, as was also the part to be played by Japan.

Propaganda and intrigue had been begun in North Africa, and German agents were busy in Afghanistan, India, and the East generally; South Africa and Ireland were being wooed, and might be won. Still other agents had been planted in the South American republics, with a view to the creation of political unrest, and of antipathy to the financial enterprises dependent on British and United States capital.

All this work was due to the genius of one man, director of the foreign side of Gestapo energies. Throughout it all he was so completely behind the scenes, so inconspicuous, that up to this present time his name has not appeared in connection with the main tasks he accomplished. Nor, at present, would it be expedient to give that name: since he was of English extraction, though not born in England, he may be designated for the purposes of this narrative (since obviously he must be defined as an entity) by the commonest of all pseudonyms —Mr. Smith. Before considering his work, a brief sketch of the man himself is necessary, since he was —and is—a rather unbelievable figure.

Born of English parents, he was in process of education at a public school in England when the last war broke out. At about the age of sixteen, he ran away to join the army: he was awarded the Military Medal and certain other decorations in addition to the usual "gongs," got captured by the Germans, escaped to Holland, and distinguished himself by his daring. After the war, being cosmopolitan rather than English, he began a series of world-wanderings, and occupied a number of important commercial posts. At some point between 1918 and the end of the 'twenties, probably early in that period, he got to Heidelberg as a student, and there so far made friends with two other students that he underwent the (to German minds) mystic ceremony of blood-brotherhood with them. These two were respectively Rolf Zimmerman, who was subsequently to become Hitler's personal aide and trusted confidant, and one whose name is not so well known, a certain Herbert Kuehnel, who became Gauleiter for the Dresden-controlled area of Bohemia, and was second only to Henlein, who had control of the Munich-controlled area adjoining the Bavarian frontier, in organizing the Sudeten Germans for the destruction of the Czecho-Slovak state.

In 1930 Smith found himself in Prague, a city that he already knew. He looked up his two blood-brothers, Kuehnel and Zimmerman, who were there at the time. For him it was no more than an enthusiastically friendly meeting of three young men: for them, it was the appearance of one who might, if he would, further the aims to which they were already devoted, which then appeared to them as the unification and emancipation of German youth, and, through that, the rescue of all Germany from the morass of anarchy in which it was sunk.

There was then no thought of world domination, or anything of the sort: they saw, and made him see, that the salvation of the nation of which they were citizens was possible through young men like him and themselves: they were, even then, trained propagandists in the doctrine of National Socialism, and they won him to belief in it. It is a marvellously specious doctrine, one that has made converts, even, of English families of high standing.

Smith was induced to go to Dresden, where he
met Captain Roehm. Then he was passed on to
Hitler himself, and his conversion was complete.
He became one of Hitler's friends, hobnobbing
with him and Streicher in Munich *bier-halles* while
as yet the Fuehrer-to-be was accessible, falling under
the spell of the man, and seeing in him then a
sincere idealist, selfless and detached from all
material rewards. Similarly, Smith did his work
with no thought of material reward: so much so
that, after he severed his connection with the Nazi
Party, he had nothing, often not enough to pay for
a night's lodging.

He met Goebbels, who, a keen judge of character,
marked him for use in the Gestapo machine even
then being planned. Even as he was being used in
it, fulfilling the purposes Goebbels and Himmler
designed him to fulfil, he assessed these immediate
masters at their real value, yet went on working—for
Hitler! He had no use for the bribes Goebbels
offered him: the work itself, the sense of accomplishment, led him on—nothing else. He knew all
the undercurrents of selfishness and intrigue that
worked to the ends of June 1934 and September
1939, and knowing them, worked with just such
cynical indifference to them as Himmler's own, to
help Goebbels while despising the man, and in the
end to assist in his relegation to the obscure background of affairs. He admired Roehm for many of
his qualities, yet watched unmoved while Hitler
himself killed that friend, for he was under the spell
of Hitler all the while. He feared Goering as one
might fear a charging elephant or a directionless
steam-roller, and at the same time, utterly detached
and impersonal, helped to direct the charging beast
along the ways favoured by its brutal instincts. All

this because he was bound to Hitler, hypnotized by
Hitler, believing in Hitler.

It was, as nearly as can be ascertained, Goebbels
who first divined the value of such a one, and the
need of him. These leaders of National Socialism
saw, and knew that they saw, the whole world
through German eyes. They had no real knowledge of foreign countries and foreign affairs: they
were German and Prussian, and on that limitation,
that failure to comprehend the mentalities of the
rest of the world, the Hohenzollern attempt at
world domination had been wrecked. Apart from
Smith with his cosmopolitan outlook, they had
only Weidemann in America, and von Papen and
von Ribbentrop in Europe, to interpret to the party
the causes underlying the policies of other than
German peoples. Had Smith accepted German
nationality when it was offered him in 1932 by
Goebbels, he might have been set over all these
three.

He did not accept, but he created and organized
the force of the Gestapo outside Germany, and on
him must rest much of the responsibility for what
has since transpired. Without his insight into the
motives actuating other than German Governments
and peoples, neither Himmler nor his Gestapo
could have been fully effective outside the Reich:
they would probably have followed the policy of
von Papen, who eventually ruined the machine
Stieber had originally built. Without Smith's work
Goebbels would not have been discredited, Goering
would not have become master of Germany as he is
to-day, there would have been no June purge in
1934, Czecho-Slovakia would not have been destroyed, nor Poland slaughtered. For the German
mind sees all things as German: even Hitler viewed

the whole world as willing to follow German leading, if only it could be proselytized through his
German youth; without the exterior, unbiassed
direction which Smith gave to Gestapo work outside the country, it must have failed.

He secured an official appointment in Prague in
1930, which justified his residence in Czecho-Slovakia before ever he met Roehm or Hitler or Goebbels.
In 1931 he was first received by Hitler in Munich,
and then was enrolled in the headquarters section
of the National Socialist Party. He had already—
instigated by Zimmerman and Kuehnel—worked
with the German minority party in Bohemia, and
had met and assisted Conrad Henlein and his
deputy, Dr. Frank, in many ways. These activities
of his had been reported to Munich, and he had
been very carefully watched, his past life investigated and checked with true Prussian thoroughness,
so that, when he eventually came to Munich, he
had been passed as trustworthy and fit for the post
then offered him.

So much for the man, Smith. Now for his work,
and for its direct and indirect results, the latter of
which are still in progress.

.   .   .   .   .

To accomplish the German penetration of
Czecho-Slovakia, Smith established his headquarters
in Prague itself. He maintained the identity connected with his official post in the country in a
small flat in a modern apartment house in Templova, a quiet, discreet sort of street in the middle of
the night-club district of the city, and only a minute
from the principal shopping and café centres of the
Graben and Vaclavsky Nemestie. His subversive
activities emanated from an entirely different point,

a large room opening on to a balcony in view of the Tyn Cathedral.

In the former apartment, Smith had been known for two years as a respectable and respected citizen, a professorial figure attached to the University: in the latter place, he was known to nobody except the son of the owner, who had arranged things for him. Even the usual police registration of guests, required by law, had been omitted in his case. The rambling old hotel was used largely as a *maison de convenance* by the patrons of the near-by cabarets and night clubs, and unobtrusive entrance could be obtained at all hours, while, as far as registration was concerned, palm oil went a long way. Here, the work that could not be done in the Templova flat without attracting attention was carried on: visitors of either sex or of any type, arriving at any hour of the day or night, attracted no attention, caused no remark.

Another centre was established at Teplitz-Schönau, a small town in the Sudetenland: its function was that of providing liaison between the Gestapo and the party organizations. The party had two bases of operation: one was in this town of Teplitz-Schönau, situated some twenty kilometres south of the Saxon frontier; this was the headquarters of Herbert Kuehnel, now made a Gauleiter for the establishment and recruiting of all youth movements. The other was at Saaz, a town occupying a strategic position between Eger and Komatau, near the Bavarian frontier; here Conrad Henlein had his headquarters, and here he centred the political work of the Sudeten German organizations, of which department he was head—directed, of course from Germany itself.

At Teplitz-Schönau provision was made for complete liaison for the various branches of work that was to penetrate every part of the Czecho-Slovak Republic, to its eventual downfall. The actual meeting-place was the apartment of a woman named Marie Heinrich, which was one of a block of flats over the Café Kreutz in Masarykstrasse—a name the German section of the population obstinately refused to recognize, still calling it Bahnhofstrasse (Station Street). This was one of the pinpricks with which Himmler himself began to set the Sudeten Germans and Czechs at loggerheads: small things of the sort were not neglected.

Here, with Marie Heinrich's apartment available, Smith established what was known both to Gestapo and party workers as the Committee of Five, who between them were to cover all the necessary departments of the work. It consisted of Smith himself, representing the Gestapo outside the Reich; Conrad Henlein, already recognized as head of all the Sudeten National Socialist Party; Herbert Kuehnel, appointed by Goebbels to organize Nazi youth movements, and at the same time to disrupt the Czech youth organization known as the "Sokol"; Frau Marie Heinrich, in charge of the formation of all Nazi women's movements in the Republic; and, lastly, a former Austrian officer of artillery, who had become an influential official of the German Social Democratic Party. His work consisted in double-crossing his own party, causing every possible dissension in it, and reporting to the committee any of its plans for the future, with a view to circumventing them.

First of the committee's objects was to settle which part of the many-sided task must be taken first; then, what activities were to be allotted to Henlein's political machine, working more or less in the open; what to Kuehnel's youth movements, and what to that most dangerous precision tool, Marie Heinrich. Himmler, considering the whole affair as a mathematical problem, had put in the forefront the disruption of the Czech Army and the economic sabotage of key industries. That at least, was Gestapo work and nothing else: the political machine could not help in it. Since Himmler had said this was the first task, first it was, although others would not be shelved while it was being done. Smith reserved it to himself, and began by consideration of the army. Could any effective means be taken so to disrupt an army of two million men that it would be unreliable either for defence or actual war? What were the factors for and against?

In the first place, the army was not class-conscious, except in its few purely Czech elements, where a rabid racial superiority complex was to be found. It was composed of the following elements, taking the figure 10 as the whole: Czechs, $3\frac{1}{2}$: Slovaks, $3\frac{1}{4}$: Germans, 3: Hungarians, Poles, Roumanians, and Ukrainians, $\frac{1}{4}$. The difficulty which the Central Government had to face, of neutralizing these racially opposing factions in the army so as to render it an effective whole, was obvious. It was overcome as far as possible by giving to every unit a slight Czech preponderance in numbers, but, since it was essential to form frontier battalions and highly mechanized units of Czechs and nothing else, no definite ratio of Czech numerical superiority could be maintained. The other elements of the whole were, if stirred up at all, mutually and even individually antagonistic, and all could be persuaded to combine to resist Czech domination. In many cases, the majority of men in a regiment could not understand the Czech language, and the resentment of such men over Czech control was a tangible thing before ever Smith started his work on them. In countries where minority problems do not exist, such a state of affairs is difficult of comprehension. Evolved and settled democracies, such as people Western Europe, are coherent; they have their internal problems and difficulties, but in the main they acknowledge Government authoriry. All South-eastern Europe is—and perhaps always will be—incoherent, a jumble of races with conflicting aims, conflicting ideals, feuds here and feuds there, inextinguishable enmities.

Some realization of the internal antipathies of Czecho-Slovakia may be gained from consideration of the fact that a Czech bank-note, paper currency of the value, say, of two shillings, was printed in five languages: Czech, Slovak, Hungarian, Russian, and German. The Gestapo, working to render these elements hostile to each other, and by these means to disrupt the army at the beginning of its work, was no mere organization of spies as these are generally known, but a superbly trained precision tool with which to accomplish military, political, economic, and industrial sabotage. Espionage in the ordinary sense was but a fraction of its activities, which covered every branch of a nation's life.

The disruption of the army was to be carried out by creating disaffection among the minorities of which it was so largely composed; it would be equally true to say that the break-up of the whole Republic was to be accomplished by the same means. The Czecho-Slovak State consisted of four provinces, Bohemia, Moravia, Slovakia, and Ruthenia or Sub-Carpathian Russia. Bohemia, in its original historical form and extent, was purely Czech, but, as the boundaries of the State were defined by the Versailles Treaty, it contained additional districts with a German population amounting to four and a half millions. Slovakia was mainly Slovak, but had had added to its original population a slice in the south which was mainly Hungarian, racially, and in the north a similar addition which was mostly peopled by Poles. Ruthenia was principally Ukrainian, with a small added Roumanian minority.

At the time of the creation of the Czecho-Slovak Republic, all these separate provinces had been promised autonomy with a Federal Government modelled on that of Switzerland. But, even prior to National Socialist machinations, German intriguers got busy in attempts at creating disaffection throughout the Republic, to such an extent that autonomous rule was seen to be impracticable for the time; the majority party, the Czechs, retained the whole machinery of government and administration in its own hands, established one central government at Prague, and—it must be added—proceeded as far as possible to eliminate all other racial languages and differences between other races and the Czechs.

The effort was foredoomed to failure—Germany saw to it that failure should result. Discontent among the minorities was fanned and not only kept alive, but increased year by year, and inasmuch as the combined minority populations totalled over 60 per cent of the whole, they made up a formidable weapon for use against the Czechs. This weapon the Gestapo proposed to use, playing upon the racial animosities of the minorities until the aims defined at Munich had been attained. Then, as planned from the very beginning, German intervention would take place, and the Republic would be carved up in accordance with Nazi policy—this with conviction, let alone knowledge, that war would not result. The Czech Republic, said Hitler, must cease to exist.

The practical work to this end was begun by Smith, then principal agent of the Gestapo for work outside Germany, who, as already noted, had an intimate knowledge of the Republic, its peoples, and conditions. His activities over the next few years were so intricate, although all directed to the one end, that it is difficult completely to separate any one section of them from the whole. So far as the army was concerned, he concentrated most of his efforts on such students as were about or almost due for military training, this not only in Prague, but in nearly every large town in the country. The minds of these youngsters were prepared by means of persistent and insidious racial propaganda, and, after they had been called up, close touch with them was maintained by letter and by personal visits to garrisons and training centres in every part of the Republic. He also secured an appointment as lecturer at the Military Academy in Prague, and there, twice a week, lectured on international history and foreign affairs to the cadet officers of the Czech Army—and it is easy to conjecture the bias and trend with which the lectures were prepared and given.

Many students of Czech nationality had also been infected with discontent over social conditions, and dissatisfaction with internal affairs of the Republic, by means of both money and propaganda and, sullen and intolerant of military discipline, they preached their doctrine of resentment and disaffection among the Czechs of their regiments. Numbers of youths of the working classes, too, had been found amenable to this propaganda: this was especially true of the horde of unemployed, whose already low standard of living was still further reduced by the absence of any form of state insurance or financial assistance. This last applied particularly to Prague. The Central Government had devoted a good deal of energy and available funds to transforming the ancient city into a modern capital, well furnished with glass and chromium milk bars and automatic restaurants before ever such things became common conveniences in London. Workless youths from all over the Republic were attracted by the somewhat meretricious glitter of the city, and thronged the streets and the magnificent embankments of the Vltava (Moldau) River in scores of thousands. The population of the city, between 1920 and 1932, had doubled itself.

No more fitting centre for the purposes of the Gestapo could have been found than existed ready to hand in this conglomerate State which had been created—this was and is the German viewpoint—as both an insult and a threat to the German people. Now the rulers of Germany planned to use the Czecho-Slovak State as an instrument for the destruction of the powers which had created it: the Gestapo was to use it not only to destroy itself, but as a training-ground and base of operations for all the external activities of that sinister organization.

Hitler referred to it as "the plague spot of Europe": the Gestapo made of it, in a different sense, the plague spot of all the civilized world. In the web of intrigue that was woven there, no single thread can be followed without touching on other threads, but the web never became tangled or confused—it was too adroitly designed for that. In Czecho-Slovakia was evolved the technique and system of training in which Gestapo agents were schooled, to be sent thence over the whole of Europe, and beyond—virtually, over all the world. The initial policy of the Gestapo consisted in reaching all elements of the Republic's population, both of Czech and minority origins, who might further its aims. Smith, as controlling authority under Himmler's direction, was a very busy man, almost ceaselessly on the move from one end of Czecho-Slovakia to the other, visiting, lecturing, inciting by implication. He kept touch with any possible English or French activities in the Republic by the establishment of both English and French clubs, over forty of which were formed in as many towns. A lecturer visited every one of these clubs frequently, with a view to keeping alive among the members the fires of disaffection. This was not a very difficult task: it complemented the work among the students, of whom the membership of these clubs was largely composed.

Some part of this lecture work was done by Smith himself, who had been registered at the French consulate as a French citizen—his command of the French language was equal with that of his own or German. The French registration came about by accident when, in completing an ordinary registration form for the Prague authorities, he had entered his place of residence as Paris, which was technically correct. With no inquiries, the form was sent to the French Consulate-general in Prague, which issued him, to his surprise, with French identity papers, and ever afterwards punctiliously sent him invitations to Embassy receptions, where he met the members of successive French Missions which at that time came to Prague from Paris. The consulate later arranged for his election as a member of the Institut Français in Prague, all of which was very useful from the Gestapo's point of view. Work among and influence on the minorities of the Republic went on, and steadily increased in the French and English academies in Prague, at the Czech Military Academy, in workers' clubs, and institutes throughout the country—the Skoda works at Pilsen, the munition works in Brno, and the shipyards at Bratislava on the Danube had their Gestapo visiting agents. The poison was spread to Ruthenia; workers' clubs with anti-Czech activities as their common object were formed at Mucacevo and Uzurvu, and in small towns among the foothills of the Carpathians. Lectures were given to sessions of Chamber of Commerce conventions, to the enormously influential Glass Manufacturers' federation of Bohemia, on the advantages of international co-operation, with heavy stress on the financial advantages of Soviet markets—every effort was made toward tangling Czecho-Slovakia with Russia in some way or other, so that Germany could allege political co-operation between the two with intent to damage the interests of the Reich.

In all the industrial areas of the country, the shortcomings of the Central Government were described—or invented. In the brown-coal-mining districts of Bohemia, tub-thumpers of the Hyde Park type told of conditions in the mining industries of England and America, with special reference to pithead baths and safety devices. At the pitchblende workings in Moravia, the workers were told of the value to the world of their labours, with emphasis on the fabulous value of even the minutest quantity of radium, to get which they toiled for such a pitiful wage while their Czech masters—etc., etc. And this was only a fraction of the work done: steadily the credit of the government was undermined, while conditions in Germany—well, as they say in the States, what have you? Politically minded, eager to learn of world-conditions, the workers of the Republic were open to Gestapo influence.

Such intercourse as Smith had with the people and institutions of the country, together with letters and reports that came in from every class and district, left no doubt that all this propaganda was producing effects on every class and in every district. He personally visited officers and men, formerly students with whom he had made close acquaintance, in the various military centres, and spent week-ends with them, in messes and in barracks. In this way he obtained comprehensive plans and descriptions of the great fortress of Frydek on the Polish frontier, constructed to guard the air corridor to Warsaw, and similarly learned the secrets of the triple ring of defences guarding Prague, and centring on and controlled from the old Austrian fortress of Theresienstadt on the north-west. He sent to Himmler, for passing on to the German General Staff, full particulars of the defences of the navigable River Elbe at Aussig and Brodenbach on the Saxon frontier. In addition he received from soldiers not only a continual stream of information, but also innumerable snapshots which were all carefully enlarged, and many of which were of value as complementary to the knowledge he had himself acquired. All this time the discontent of minorities in the army was being fostered; they were, when possible, set one against another, and all against the Czechs.

Meanwhile the work of organizing the Sudeten Germans went on, directed from Teplitz-Schönau, and the political developments continued under direction of the Nazi Sudeten chiefs at Saaz and Eger. The material on which Nazi propaganda was used was pliable enough: in a normal way, it consisted of peaceable, politically sluggish South Germans, who like all their kind were capable of being regimented and ordered about, and in fact rather liked that sort of thing. The Czechs had neglected the organization of these Sudetens into a political machine; they had, too, rather put Czech interests before those of the Sudeten Germans, even insisting that purely Czech industries should rank equally with those of the non-Czech part of the population in the Sudetenland. Nazi propagandists preached and insisted that this was intolerable, and, as always, set to work to inflame the youth of the district, and organize the women—reference to this work has already been made.

Conrad Henlein, leader of the Sudeten Nazi movement, formed a strong *bloc* of Nazi deputies in the Central Parliament, and the Czech Government realized the possible dangers of Berlin-directed influence, but saw no means of controverting it. They tried a few rather ineffectual measures; one of them was that of prohibiting the wearing of Nazi uniforms: Sudeten and imported German youths, at that, took to wearing white stockings as marks of their political leanings—an affectation which, with the baggy plus-fours they usually affected, showed up wonderfully. Then the Government stopped both the sale and manufacture of white stockings throughout the Republic, so Sudeten Nazi youth took to smuggling. It would all have been silly, had it not been so deadly in earnest.

The whole country, after a year or two of Gestapo work, was riddled with clubs and societies, each of

which was a centre of social and political unrest;
those belonging to each minority suspected all the
others, but all combined in subversive activities
against the loyalist Czechs, who were rigorously
excluded from them and forestalled in any attempts
at interference. The Deutsches Haus in Prague,
situated in the Graben, one of the principal streets,
was like a fortress. Its street frontage contained only
one small window and a pair of enormously strong
wooden gates, with a small wicket for individual
entries. Inside, round a large central court, were
buildings containing basement beer halls, restaurants, gymnasia, meeting-rooms, conference
rooms, headquarter apartments, and roof-gardens,
all given up to Nazi activities.

In Teplitz-Schönau, the Committee of Five set up
by the Gestapo to co-ordinate all the elements of
disaffection met at frequent intervals at Number 23,
Mazarykstrasse, over the Café Kreuz. It had a discreet side entrance, overshadowed by the high,
glass-doored side of the Kaffeehaus, and the interior
was well and tastefully furnished. It formed a fitting background for Marie Heinrich, who at the age
of forty-two was not only a very clever woman, but
a charming one as well, with all the wit of a
Viennese and the chic of a Parisienne—at the same
time she was as hard as chilled steel behind the
attractive façade. No woman in all Europe could
have been more fitted for the work assigned to her.

She formed the League of German Mothers who
were pledged to support National Socialism and
Hitler, and to influence their families in every way
to a like end. She herself said before the year 1936
ended that there was not a German mother in the
Sudetenland who did not belong to the League, and
in that she said no less than truth.

The work of the member of the Social Democratic Party who had been roped in to betray it, whose "German nature had been appealed to by Henlein," with promises of high reward when the Fuehrer came to Czecho-Slovakia—if the traitor did his work, of course—and threats of what would happen to him, his family, and all that was his, if he did not, had been successful in accomplishing results: both the Social Democratic and Communist parties were splitting, becoming futile.

Herbert Kuehnel's youth organizations grew and flourished; centres complete with gymnasia and recreational facilities, based on the principle of the Reich Brown Houses, were established throughout the Sudetenland, and in most districts eighty per cent and over of the available youths had been enrolled. By youths was meant all between the ages of fifteen and twenty-five, the impressionable years. A large proportion of these belonged in families where the fathers and elders were of Social Democratic or Communist tendencies, but, in accordance with the Nazi principles of propaganda, it was calculated that the combined influences of mothers and young people would deflect the head of the family from any political allegiance which—as they pointed out and insisted—would render him liable to heavy punishment when the Fuehrer should come. Even if he persisted in his evil courses, it could only be a half-hearted allegiance.

Girls and young women were enrolled in their own organization, which was created and staffed by Marie Heinrich, with just as much thoroughness and success as that prevailing in the youths' and mothers' movements. It was found, in fact, that the girls displayed more enthusiastic and even fanatical allegiance to Hitler than did the boys, and any youths who evinced lukewarmness in regard to the "cause" were whipped up to the mark by girl friends and mothers. Week-end youth hostels were established all along the line of the Saxon and Bohemian frontiers of the Sudetenland, deep in the woods and wilds of the mountains—the Hartz Mountains of many a romantic and eerie legend. Here the members of the youth movement spent their week-ends and holidays, efficiently organized, absorbing the beauties of nature and National Socialist propaganda, both with zest and thoroughness, while they ascertained the exact positions of frontier defences, guard houses, and patrol beats, for the benefit of the Gestapo.

All this was not for nothing. In 1937, these same youth hostels were used as a means of getting across the frontier from the Reich arms and ammunition in vast quantities, with which, as the culmination of the Gestapo work in Czecho-Slovakia, the Sudeten youth were armed. Every form of help that could be given to each other by the two departments controlled by Henlein and Kuehnel was exchanged, and it is easy to see that Kuehnel's work, affecting youths as it did, gave Henlein a superiority of voting power over any other party.

The general instructions given to Henlein for the political conduct of his party were drawn up by Goebbels and Himmler, and conveyed to him at Saaz by Smith, head of external Gestapo work at the time. They were, in effect, that Henlein should make modest demands on the Central Government, and then secretly sabotage all offers of conciliation made by it, using the other minorities to accomplish this. The resulting failure of negotiations was then to be publicly announced as another betrayal of the oppressed Germans of the Sudetenland by the Czechs, and a further breaking of their promises. Negotiations were then to be reopened, backed by threats of the Fuehrer's intervention, and with demands going a little farther. This was to be repeated *ad infinitum*, but no conclusion or settlement was ever to be reached. No alliance of any kind was to be made with the Slovak minority, but they were to be given to understand the method of working, and encouraged to imitate it. The object of all this was not merely that of creating internal dissensions in the Government, but also that of representing it to the world as obstructionist and persistently oppressive, willing to accept help from France, Roumania, the Soviets, or anywhere else, in order to preserve the dominance of the Czech element. It was to be represented always that the policy of the Czech Government was fundamentally Communistic, and therefore a threat to the Reich. Everything possible must be done to create and foster ill-will between Czecho-Slovakia and Poland, and in this the Gestapo helped by directing ceaseless propaganda in the Polish minority area of Teschen, "until the Fuehrer came."

This, in outline, was the political programme which Henlein followed, reporting as his opinion that decisive results would be obtained by 1936 or 1937. By 1935, the Social Democratic and Communist parties in the Sudetenland were dismayed at their dwindling membership and resulting futility. The Communist Party no longer even attempted to hold open-air demonstrations or display red flags. Instead, every open square and park was utilized for the demonstrations of Nazi youth, with gymnastic displays, bands, and loud-speakers. Since the National Socialist colours were prohibited, they displayed in the form of belts, pocket handkerchiefs, or as part of the design of women's hats or girls' blouses, the red, black, and gold of imperial Germany.

Through all this moved the ever-active figure of Smith, the Gestapo chief of operations in the country. His work included liaison between Czecho-Slovakia and Germany, and a score of times a year he went to Dresden, Munich, or Berlin to report on the progress of the work and take part in the conferences with Goebbels and Himmler, from which emanated some fresh or more intensified activity. In his Gestapo headquarters in Prague, an unending succession of carefully selected young men of every class, every profession and trade, were interviewed by him. Among them were workers already trained and planted in every key industry of the Republic, all highly skilled workers who would carry out industrial espionage as long as necessary, and be ready to take their parts in industrial sabotage if the climax of the campaign called for it. Others who kept touch in this same fashion with Gestapo headquarters were men in or intimately connected with the provincial and municipal administrations of the State. Smith had first made contact with them in the course of his social and professional activities, and now such as appeared likely to be of use were drawn in and employed. These formed the means by which still another item of the Munich programme could be accomplished, wherever the Henlein and Keuhnel sections of the organization could not operate; this was the penetration of provincial and municipal administrative bodies by means of bribes, graft, and, when necessary, threats. All the interior administration of the country was shown by the Gestapo as—and to some extent actually was—

biassed in favour of the Czech-born elements, and, in minority towns and provinces, the strictest economy was enforced by the Czech Government. Thus, it was pointed out and hammered home by Gestapo agents, the minority districts, in which many of the richest industrial areas were situated, were disproportionately taxed for the support of the poorer Czech-inhabited parts of the country. With this suggestion of unfair taxation, combined with a score more grievances, manufactured or otherwise, against the Czechs, it was not difficult to get men from every centre to visit the Gestapo headquarters and hear what could be done toward bringing about a (from the propaganda-doctored minority point of view) more equitable state of affairs.

They were tempted, bribed, or blackmailed into consenting to play their parts in disorganizing the administrations, and, from time to time, given that part of their reward which was advanced against the coming of the Fuehrer, who—they were assured and convinced—would give the rest. What he actually gave, even to such leaders as Henlein and Kuehnel, let alone the rank and file, is now history.

By 1936, the forces of disaffection at work in the army and throughout every department of the State were tangible realities, and comprised a power evident, even then, as a grave danger to the continuing existence of the Republic. The Central Government was aware of this, but it looked to the Western powers for help, and did its best to maintain Czech institutions and influence in face of the carefully organized and fomented antagonisms striking to bring about downfall—at the behest and in the interests of Nazi Germany. By 1937 the Government realized its helplessness and inability to master the forces gathered and still gathering against it.

Still other sections of Gestapo work had to be completed before the ultimate blow was struck. These were planned and carried out as a result of Goebbels' anxiety over the accumulation of plenty of evidence to show that any decisive action the Reich might take would be fully justified not only by ineptitude, but by treachery and actual plotting against the Reich as well. This anxiety of his was due to the affair of the Reichstag fire in 1933, and the fright into which he had been thrown when evidence on which he had counted for implication of the Communist Party had been suppressed by Goering and Himmler, to the Herr Doctor's utter discomfiture and loss of prestige. Such a thing, he determined, must not happen again, especially over so important an affair as the sabotage of a republic.

In connection with the manufacture of such evidence, since it did not exist, certain Gestapo leaders set to work to show that the Czech Government, and commercial interests acting on its behalf, were engaged in both political and economic intrigue with a view to the detriment of the Reich. For this purpose London and Paris had to be visited, so as to obtain documentary evidence implicating English and French commercial concerns in Central European intrigues directed from Czecho-Slovakia. From 1934 to 1938 this business went on, the object being that of securing documents which, supported by forged additions—even the seals of the Czech Republic were forged—and added to other "evidence" that Himmler had contrived, linked up Czecho-Slovak, English, and French commercial activities with Soviet Russia, the whole designed as injury to Germany.

All this fabricated justification of Hitler's policy in regard to Czecho-Slovakia, apparently incontestable, was held ready to offer to the world at the right moment: quite probably some if not all of it was put before Mr. Chamberlain at Godesberg and Munich. It had a further purpose—that of creating suspicion, if no more, between England and France, and rendering it probable, if not certain, that both countries would hold their hands when Germany struck the final blow at Czecho-Slovakia, since that country was implicated with Soviet Russia in plots for the economic detriment of Germany.

Frequent visits were also necessary to Poland, to Roumania, Austria, Jugoslavia, Swizterland, and the Low Countries. The big Packard car of the Gestapo control in Prague became known at the frontiers of some of these countries, but the real activities of its occupants remained unsuspected, since their ostensible missions were so soundly planned as to form guarantees of probity. The minority situation in Jugoslavia complicated Gestapo work in that country with what was being done in Czecho-Slovakia; as will be detailed in its place, batches of Croat youths were selected and enrolled in Prague universities, to be trained for Nazi Party and Gestapo work with the assistance of the Nazi Party machinery and the youth organizations of the Sudetenland.

Side by side with all these activities in the Czech Republic, the work of selecting and training agents for Gestapo work outside Germany was planned and conducted. It had been decided at the initial conferences in Munich that these agents should not be of purely German origin, that they should be very highly trained after careful selection from the mass of available material. This was not because of reluctance to use Germans for the purpose because they *were* Germans, but with realization that the German mind was too rigid; the ineradicable quality which causes everything to be viewed from a German standpoint would result in work of doubtful value, since it would not be objective enough for the technique of the reconstituted German Secret Service.

Thus the men had to be found and shaped— "created" was the word that had been used—before work could be begun outside Czecho-Slovakia. The immediate need was for agents who could be sent to Central European countries, to the Balkans and Poland; later, others would be required, rather differently trained, for Western Europe and the United States. These latter, it was realized, would be called on to work in an atmosphere completely alien to that which they knew, among people of a very different mentality from that of Eastern Europeans, and using languages strange to them— languages in which they must be made proficient. Also their training must be wider in its scope, and thus would take longer than that needed for work in Eastern and South-eastern Europe.

The field of choice was wide. Among the German minority of the Sudetenland were many suitable youths of mixed Austrian and Czech descent, of excellent education, and accustomed almost from childhood to the restless and almost purposeless wandering which is such a prominent characteristic of Central European peoples. So much so is this the case that it is not uncommon to meet a middle-aged peasant woman, complete with her basket in which is packed a week's provisions, setting out in a dreary, comfortless third-class railway coach on some journey of incredible length and difficulty, perhaps to see some migrated relative, and perhaps for little reason beyond the desire to see a country of which she has heard: younger adventurers of the kind do not even take baskets, but trust to luck and so cross Europe.

There were, also, the minorities of all the Central European countries among whom to choose, and those finally selected were not only taken from minorities—with their perpetual feuds and grievances—but were in practically every case of mixed blood. Croat–Hungarian, Slovak–Austrian, Czech–Austrian, German–Polish, Croat–Italian, and so forth, always with care that there was a strain of German or pro-German origin in the subject chosen.

An exception was made in the case of agents designed for work in America: there, they would require a thorough knowledge of Czech for meeting their—supposedly—Czech compatriots in the States, and, for this, Bulgarians were chosen. All Slav languages are so similar in structure that a little practice makes any two of them interchangeable, and a Bulgarian can easily and quickly adapt his own tongue so as to pass as a Czech, possibly of border origin.

All the required agents were found, youths of twenty years or thereabouts who were amenable to Nazi influence, soaked up the Nazi doctrine, and then were enlisted for Gestapo work—though not without a great deal of careful examination, selection, and rejection of material that proved unsuitable or in any way fell below the required standard.

The four Bulgarians who eventually went to America may be taken as samples of the material from which Gestapo agents were fashioned. Chosen

in the first place by the Gestapo chief of external
work, who was already acquainted with several
families in Sofia, they had been educated in France
and Italy, and had also undergone a course at the
American College in Stamboul, which is staffed by
American professors who give all instruction in
English—American-English, that is. They were
thus multi-lingual, speaking French, Italian, and
German, and colloquial American, all before any
one of them had reached the age of twenty. They
possessed all the qualities which, in the view of the
Gestapo, were necessary as groundwork for their
training: their outlook on life was cosmopolitan
and very little limited by any national ideas or conceptions; their attitude as regards the whole field of
conventional ethics was definitely un-moral; they
had, at the end of their 'teens, no convictions,
fewer susceptibilities, and their consciences would
never incite to remorse, nor would the keenness of
their mentalities ever be dulled by any considerations of *meum* and *tuum*—rather was the contrary
the case. In spite of all this, there was in them all
the queer little streak of unrestful reaching-out—it
is a quality impossible to define more clearly—on
which the Gestapo knew so well how to play.

The four, chosen in Sofia, were sent for a
refresher course to the American College in Stamboul, and thence went to Czecho-Slovakia. There
a training centre had to be established for these and
other potential Gestapo workers, one that must be
very efficient, and at the same time inconspicuous:
the Gestapo could arrange for efficiency; the rest
was left to the chiefs of the Nazi Party in the
Sudetenland, and Herbert Kuehnel found the place,
in Teplitz-Schönau, his own headquarters, where
was situated the old Austrian Imperial School of

Ceramics—Vienna is one of the world's great centres of the ceramic craft. The Teplitz-Schönau school is the only one of its kind in Europe, and at that time it was receiving students from many different countries. Owing to currency regulations and political difficulties it was not patronized as much as under the Imperial régime, but its reputation was still high, the value of credentials issued by it unquestioned everywhere, and, although it was in the very centre of the Sudeten Nazi Party activities, it was regarded as above suspicion by the Czech authorities. The then director of the school was one of Kuehnel's disciples, an ardent National Socialist, and he agreed without question to Kuehnel's proposal to enrol certain young men in the school and issue them with all necessary papers to declare them students in the School of Ceramics. He also agreed that certain additional professors, nominated by Kuehnel, should be added to the staff, and that all members of that staff who could not be implicitly trusted should be dismissed.

Thus was the training centre formed, and the first batch of trainees were enrolled. As they came from Italy, Croatia, Hungary, and Roumania, as well as from Slovakia, they excited no comment and called forth no official questioning; their enrolment for a course in ceramics was sufficient, backed as it was with the papers of origin and identity supplied to them all by the Gestapo.

Their training was begun in accordance with Nazi requirements, and included the specialized elements of applied psychology in its most fundamental form, which Gestapo work would involve. With this was combined intensive practical training in National Socialist propaganda work, and Gestapo methods and technique throughout Czecho-Slovakia and the neighbouring countries. In all, some ninety-six youths passed through this school between 1934 and 1937, and so rigorous had been the preliminary examination of them all that in no one case was the selection of them at fault. They form, at this present time, the complete Gestapo staff for external operations, are scattered throughout the world, and are implicitly, completely trusted by Himmler as representative of their employers.

The course of training in the first years, as given to the urgently needed agents for Poland and South-eastern Europe, was of necessity limited to nine or ten months. The party sent to France underwent nearly eighteen months of fitting for their task, and the four Bulgarians ultimately sent to the United States received well over two years of training, inclusive of their refresher course at Stamboul. As all of them became available, they were absorbed into the Gestapo organization and taken to be personally initiated into the territory in which they had to operate, provided with all the necessary papers, identities, and passports, and given all the introductions, contacts, and detailed knowledge of conditions in front of them that the Gestapo had collected for their benefit. Only the four trained for work in the U.S.A. went to their task without personal guidance by some Gestapo chief.

The presence of foreign students at the School of Ceramics was rendered still less conspicuous by the fact that it was not the only cause of cosmopolitanism in Teplitz-Schönau. For centuries the town has been a "bad" for the cure of rheumatism, for which it has received sufferers from all over the world. Adapted for this purpose, it has an attractive atmosphere of cafés, flowers, and music; there are open rose-gardens overlooked by café terraces, a profusion of Japanese cherry-trees, and there is every variety of amusement, including two theatres. It is, too, one of the centres of the old Gablonz industry—necklaces, and a variety of ornaments and trinkets made of glass and *diamante*; buyers and business men from all over Europe and America visit Teplitz.

Strangers in the town, therefore, passed unnoticed; they might be there for the "*kur*," or on business connected with Gablonz or glass. For this reason many of the Gestapo visitors were received in Teplitz-Schönau rather than in Prague—including, on several occasions, a number of Japanese visitors who, arriving *via* Italy, came to discuss affairs in America and the Far East with the Gestapo control.

This part of the work was linked up with Gestapo activities for the dismemberment and absorption of Czecho-Slovakia, in that the potential agents under training were able to get practical insight to the complicated, tortuous type of work they themselves would have to do, each in his allotted sphere of action. Meanwhile the series of operations that was to crash the Credit Anstalt in Vienna and disrupt the financial and economic life of Austria was pursued. By 1937, Hitler could have reached out and taken Czecho-Slovakia; he delayed only because, in his scheme of things, Austria must come first, though all the fires that had been lighted in the Czech Republic had burned almost to their appointed ends.

Every member of the Council of Five had brought his particular task to the verge of complete accomplishment. Henlein had succeeded in undermining the stability of the Central Government; Kuehnel had completely organized the youth of the Sudetenland, and they had been most efficiently armed with machine-guns, rifles, grenades, and almost limitless ammunition brought in by way of those youth hostels that dotted the slopes of the Sudeten Mountains; Marie Heinrich's task of organizing the women and girls was completed; the Social Democrat who had been persuaded to sabotage the Communist Party as well as his own had done his work so well that in the remnants remaining of these two parties were none but middle-aged and old men, and even these were now apprehensive of the fate awaiting them "when the Fuehrer came"—as, all saw now, come he would. In Room No. 9 of the Hotel Ungeld in Prague, the Gestapo headquarters, work had been done that fitted near on a thousand skilled workers into the industrial and commercial life of the country, every one of them ready to begin sabotage if and when the word was given.

The internal disruption of the Army was completed: it could not survive the process of complete mobilization for purposes of war. Slovakia was ready for revolt if Germany offered her help. No fortification in the country had any secrets from the German General Staff, which had already, after prolonged and exact calculation based on information supplied by the Gestapo, informed Hitler that the German armed forces could reach Prague within twelve hours of crossing the frontier.

Over fifty per cent of the municipal authorities of Bohemia and Moravia had been corrupted by and were subservient to Henlein, and the Gestapo had achieved a similar corruption among the members of the Czech financial administration, while industry and commerce were undermined by Nazi influences, and even the courts of justice were used to further Gestapo aims. Little remained to be done: the shadow of the swastika was over Prague, over the great palace on Hradcany Hill that housed the President, and, as if clouding the brilliant sunlight of summer, 1937, that same shadow brooded over the Vaclavsky Nemestie, *Die Graben*, the flower-covered heights of Letna, the graceful pile of the Parliament building, the imposing embankments of the Vltava, and the placid river itself. Before that summer ended, Prague was a city of fear.

The final tragedy—tragedy of Munich and Hitler's treacherous, lying, cynical policy and its success, rather than that of the doomed Republic—is history, and needs no recital here. It was in keeping with the ruthless, conscienceless, utterly unscrupulous Gestapo work that preceded and rendered it a possibility.

V

WORK IN POLAND

THE technique used to bring about the downfall of the Czecho-Slovak Republic was applied to all the Eastern and South-eastern European States in which the existence of racial minorities promised results. That is to say, in every country between the Alps on the west and the Soviet frontier on the east, with the exceptions of Austria, Hungary, and Bulgaria, which called for other modes of operation.

In describing the methods used and the results obtained, it is not possible to observe a strict chronological sequence. Countries were not taken in sequence, but step by step as the Gestapo organization for foreign work was formed and enlarged. Thus, in dealing with events in Poland, it must be remembered that Gestapo penetration of that country was begun as early as 1933, and was continued side by side with activities in many other countries, all originated and for some years controlled by Smith from his headquarters in Prague, and not from the Reich—to which, of course, he was directly responsible, though given a very free hand in view of the insight which he possessed and the Prussian mind knew that it lacked—insight into non-German mentalities, and ability to foresee the reactions to any move that might be made.

In the light of what was accomplished in the Czecho-Slovak Republic, as outlined in the preceding chapter, it will be seen that in Poland there

were many parallels. As far as the racial composition of the country was concerned, the population
of the east and south was almost exclusively White
Russian and Ukrainian, by no means to be confused
with each other; both were fiercely nationalist in
outlook and hopes, and thus were automatically
opposed to Polish domination. In the north, the
separated minorities of Lithuania, centred round
Vilna, presented admirable material (this is from the
Gestapo viewpoint) for anti-Polish propaganda
work. The Eastern provinces, Silesia, Danzig, and
Memel, were very largely German. The new port of
Gdynia, created by Poland and separated from
Polish influences by the largely German Pomorz
provinces of the Corridor, was nervous and
barely sure of a continuing existence, with Danzig
and its German elements just across the way. The
purely Polish portion of the State, corresponding
roughly with the limits of the former Grand Duchy
of Warsaw, was determined at all costs and by all
means to preserve the State as a whole in the form
and extent granted in 1920, although, at that time,
the map-makers of Versailles had urged the accept-
ance of a frontier in accordance with the "Curzon
Line," with its key strategic points ranging from
Vilna in the north, through Brest-Litovsk to
Lemberg (Lwow) in the south-east.

Apart from all other provinces in which racial
minorities might be used by Germany to make
trouble, the most dangerous to Polish policy was
the former Hungarian province of Eastern Galicia,
south of Lemberg, with its oilfields, coal-mines,
industrial works, and the fortress of Przemysl
which controls the passes of the Carpathians. In
addition to this ever-present possibility of disruption, the Warsaw Government had Germany,

Hungary, and Roumania to fear, while Soviet Russia was a possible cause of apprehension, and bitter hostility existed between Poland and Czecho-Slovakia. Add to this the fact that the administration had in it a considerable Jewish element, and it becomes apparent that the Gestapo had very fertile soil in which to plant and cultivate.

The numbers of the racial minorities were formidable. There were about ten millions of White Russians and Ukrainians, between three and four million Hungarians and Germans, probably a million or so of the mixed, non-Polish races of the Baltic States round Vilna, and some four million Jews—all these in a total population of between thirty-five and forty millions. This was the state and composition of Poland at the time of the beginning of Gestapo activities.

These facts, little realized to west of Germany, must be accepted if the course of events in Eastern Europe, and the part played in them by the Gestapo, are to be fully understood. So little of the Treaty of Versailles remains to-day that it is possible to criticize it: to the German mind, it was not so much unjust as a means of causing trouble, of upsetting all Europe in order to further German aims. Had it been rigidly insisted on, had Germany been stopped from ever beginning its present campaign for world domination with the acquisition of the Saar, the new frontiers defined at Versailles would in time have become lines of effective resistance; minorities would have acquiesced in government by majorities, as those governments grew stable and accepted the principle of equal justice for all—as for their own sakes they would, if left to work out their destinies.

But Prussianism, given its chance, seized on National Socialism as its weapon, destroyed the

Versailles Treaty bit by bit, eventually to stand forth again as a potent enemy of Democracy and the personal freedom for which it stands. It used the Nazi Party in every case, and the Gestapo where necessary, to create discord. The results of its work in Poland, in Roumania, and in Jugoslavia cannot be explained without comprehension of the existences and extents of the racial minorities in these countries, through which the Gestapo worked.

As for the West, France, England, and the United States, the technique was altered to a finer —and, it may be said, deadlier—style, with a view to influence on the internal affairs of the countries concerned, and to the accomplishment of military objectives—as will be shown in their places. In the East, minorities were all-important for the work.

By the end of 1934, branches of the National Socialist Party had been established throughout all Western Poland, among the German minorities settled there, and among the East Galicians of German origin, who formerly had considered themselves as belonging under the government of Hungary: more especially were the settlements at Lemberg and Przemysl proselytized, and brought under Nazi influence. These activities were controlled from Dresden, under Captain Roehm's supervision.

Danzig was a separate entity, controlled directly from Goering's offices in Munich in the first place, and, later, from the Chancellory in Berlin. Such work as had to be done in Memel and Lithuania was also under this latter centre. The methods used were the usual propaganda movements through the youth of the areas concerned, and the undermining of all democratic institutions by the judicious planting inside them of agents who, to outward

seeming loyal and even enthusiastic, in reality
seized on every chance to set member against
member, and bring discredit on the institutions as a
whole. This was Nazi Party work, distinct from
that of the Gestapo: it was the sort of dirty work in
which the ex-artillery officer and political figure in
Prague proved so efficient in the undermining of
political institutions in Czecho-Slovakia.

The Gestapo came in where Eastern Poland was
concerned. It sapped at the Central Government in
Warsaw with more or less success, working to
influence the political and economic policy by
antagonizing minority sections and, in particular,
undermining by any means whatever the financial
power of the Jews. Gestapo agents, trained at the
school in Teplitz-Schönau which was supported by
the Czech Government as a school of ceramics,
were sent throughout Eastern Poland and established in Warsaw. They worked as their counter-
parts were working among the minorities in Czecho-
Slovakia, and as others worked in Roumania and
Jugoslavia, and they achieved similar results. These
included alienation from the Polish Government of
White Russian and Ukrainian minorities, and also
of the Vilna section of non-Polish population. This
work was so thoroughly done that some arrangement
with Russia concerning the future status of these
minorities became essential: by 1937 at latest, both
Germany and Russia as represented by Stalin began
to regard a fourth partition of Poland as a necessity.

It is apparent to-day that such attempts as were
made by England and France to influence Soviet
policy were utterly futile: from the first, they were
never taken seriously by Moscow, and had no
chance of success. To what extent English and
French statesmen realized this is matter for con-

jecture. It may be that, of all the democratic statesmen, Chamberlain alone realized how much had
been done to bring totalitarian and Russian interests into alignment, and that realization may
account for his reluctance to enter on war as long as
an alternative—any alternative—appeared possible.
In Germany, up to this present time, he is regarded
as one who might see the wisdom of acquescing in
Prussian aims, but is so subservient to Socialist and
Liberal influences in this country as to be driven by
them, even into war.

The penetration of Poland, and influence toward
antagonizing the minorities of the country by
trained Gestapo agents, was regarded as no difficult
task. The work proceeded along the lines that had
brought success in Czecho-Slovakia, and was helped
by the conflicting currents which affected the policy
of the central administration. Those who worked
for the national interests of Poland—such men as
Colonel Beck and Marshal Smigly-Rydz—were
actuated by purely patriotic motives; they had no
idea of the financial intrigues which corrupted the
provincial and even the central administration.
Beck, too, was so genuinely desirous of the welfare
of the Polish State that he delayed action too long;
if he had come down definitely, while there was
still time, on either side, the course of events would
have not been what it is to-day: Beck is a Pole, and
in essence the Polish mentality is akin to the
Russian—bargain and bargain to the last second,
the last fraction of a second. By this both Beck and
Poland fell.

None of these considerations were overlooked by
the Gestapo in the furtherance of its work; they
were analysed and used to definite purpose and
concrete effect. Here, also, the Gestapo for the first

time arranged to co-operate with the military
authorities of the Reich and engaged in military
espionage. Not as was done almost simultaneously
in Czecho-Slovakia, but on a definitely military basis
and embodying a new military technique, worked
out and detailed by General von Fritsch, then
Commander-in-Chief of the German Army. The
scheme adopted was part of the technique of the
Army, which was to be applied to all "Blitzkriege"
or "lightning wars." It was to be applied, if necessary, to Poland in the first place, and then to France
and England, and was designed not only for the effectiveness which was foreseen as rendering the German
striking power irresistible, but also still further to
glorify Goering in his command of the air forces.

The plan was, in effect, to immobilize the land
forces of an opponent by confronting its land frontier with an overwhelming display of force, thus
compelling the opponent to concentrate all his
power to defend the frontier. A preponderance of
air force would then be used to break all civil
resistance and destroy moral. It was—still is—to the
German mind an effective reply to the technique of
the blockade, which is considered England's most
effective and most favoured weapon.

Gestapo agents, therefore, mapped out Poland
to the west of Warsaw with meticulous exactness;
every mile of road and railway, every junction,
siding, industrial centre, etc., was most clearly and
completely surveyed and marked in. Not only was
the exact position of every rail depot, factory, road,
and all the rest, shown and measured, but the
requisite quantity of explosive for its destruction
was calculated and set down for the guidance of the
military chiefs.

The part played in all this by von Fritsch, then

Commander-in-Chief, has its interest, especially in view of his ultimate fate. General Baron von Fritsch was Goering's tool, and, when Goering was intriguing up to 1934 for the overthrow of the military *bloc* to ensure his own command of the Army and control of Prussia, he put Fritsch in the place of the then Commander-in-Chief, General Baron von Hammerstein-Equord. He promised von Fritsch the rank of Field-Marshal General, and complete command, with no intention whatever of keeping the promise.

Von Fritsch was an artillery expert and a military strategist not only of the highest order, but also with a completely modern mind. In this ability lay a danger that Goering feared: when von Fritsch had been sucked dry, Goering decided, he must go. In conjunction with the Gestapo—Smith, occupied as he was then in Czech affairs, yet found time to consult with the General and direct the Gestapo co-operation—Fritsch worked out the technique to be employed in all German military operations, the "lightning" tactics used against Poland with such effectiveness, with the country prepared in advance by the Gestapo as, in the middle of last century, Stieber had prepared Austria for the army commanded by von Moltke. This same technique is intended for use, in a form adapted to the differing conditions, against France and England, and nothing, literally, has been left to chance.

In 1935, von Fritsch was personally congratulated by Hitler, since his completed plans were so satisfactory as to secure unmixed approval, and was given Cabinet rank. Early in 1938 Goering managed to displace him, together with Field-Marshal von Blomberg, and awarded the command of the army to its present Commander-in-Chief, von Brauchitsch. Twice, prior to this, Goering had attempted to dispose of the man he no longer wanted: at his (Goering's) instigation, Himmler had brought charges of immoral conduct with soldiers against von Fritsch in 1935, when Hitler personally quashed them and, defying Goering in his defence of the General, made von Fritsch an "Excellency." But, in the end, Goering had his way, and von Brauchitsch took over the command.

Hitler, now so far in Goering's power that he could do nothing effectively, made a gesture of defiance. He addressed a message of congratulation to von Fritsch for his work with the army and for the Reich, and made him honorary Colonel of the Twelfth Artillery Regiment, with the ineffective rank of Colonel-General. Von Fritsch's death outside Warsaw in September of 1939, in the midst of the country he had planned so effectively to destroy, may be considered as due to one of two causes: either he deliberately sought death as the easiest way out, or, more probably, Goering made a final and successful effort, through the agency of Himmler, to dispose of an outworn tool that might prove dangerous.

An excerpt from the funeral oration delivered by von Brauschitsch, as reported in the Daily Telegraph of September 27th, 1939, is worth quoting. "He was," said the present Commander-in-Chief, "one of the best men the army ever had. In 1934 the Fuehrer entrusted him with the task of forging the German Army in accordance with National Socialist principles. . . . There is one quality of his which I wish to emphasize—his loyalty to his Fuehrer, the people, and the army. He was as loyal as a rock."

He was broken on a rock—that of Goering's ruthless ambition.

VI

ROUMANIA

IN its opening stages, Gestapo work in Roumania was no more than a little leaven which, in time, should work to permeate the whole. It consisted of two agents and no more, sent to the country in 1933. They had been trained in Czecho-Slovakia for their work, and may be regarded as a pair of delicately fashioned and highly finished tools, shaped as they were for every branch of the work, able for all contingencies. Apparently a couple of keen young business men, they established themselves in the Callea Victorei, Bucharest, in 1933, with unimpeachable credentials, and holding genuine agencies for trade in Roumania. One represented French wine interests; the other was concerned in the importation and sale of electrical wares, with a strong show of radio receivers and accessories. Pleasant young chaps, out to entertain as well as to be entertained, and, evidently, very prosperous. Gestapo work is never hindred by considerations of finance: it is far too important an adjunct of Nazi policy for cheese-paring.

These two missionaries set to their real work, and attracted to themselves a number—as many as they wanted—of Roumanian helpers, mainly of the sort that can be found in most countries—certainly in all Eastern European states!—with whom nothing counts as much as easy money. Each parasite of this type who looked like being useful was bought at once, and his knowledge and social and political

175

connections utilized to swell the stream of information of every sort that flowed toward Gestapo headquarters in Berlin. And, as is always the case, the information was checked and counter-checked: if any one of these agents proved unreliable or in any way inefficient, his pay was stopped, and he was discarded: what he had already done was enough to keep his mouth shut in quarters where he might have done damage: if it were not, there were methods of bringing pressure to bear on him; for one thing, it is usually possible to forestall an informer, and thus to discredit him.

The internal constitution of Roumania lent itself just as completely to Gestapo work as did those of Czecho-Slovakia and Poland. It was, in fact, found easier to use the methods of the organization in this country, controlled as it was by a semi-autocratic government retaining many of the forms and practices of a century ago, than in the democratic republics with their more open forms of control. This became particularly evident in that branch of the work which consisted in putting ceaseless political pressure on the Government, which was done more and more as adherents were drawn to the Nazi cause.

As usual, the Gestapo made a careful survey of the ground, and estimated the quality of the material with which it could work, as well as forming an estimate of conditions in Roumania, and then considering what modifications of its methods were necessary in such a country. The political factors were summed up, economic and industrial possibilities were surveyed, weighed and measured and card-indexed, and, in addition, the Gestapo supplied specially trained agents to make a complete military survey, again working in close touch with the German Army staff.

Political activities came first. The pair of agents in Bucharest bought, cajoled, and suborned where and how they could, and their opportunities were legion: as any commercial interest from outside trying to operate in the country, finds to its cost, nearly every municipal administration has its corruptible figures, and the Central Government itself is not free of them. Add to this the fact that Nazi influences were already at work, to such an extent that a party was growing up in the country, and it will be seen that the pair in the Callea Victorei had plenty of raw material from which to fashion other agents. Perfectly trained themselves, they became trainers: the leaven did its work.

A summary of the conditions in which the work was done becomes necessary. The aristocracy and landowners of the country are completely apart from the mass of the people, and the great majority of the peasant class in Roumania have few rights and a very low status. Territorial acquisitions from Versailles are, to put it frankly, unnatural, and by reason of them the Central Government is, up to to-day, faced with the problem of holding its new possessions against the jealousies of surrounding states. Bulgaria has never ceased to agitate for the return of the Dobrudja to what Bulgarians consider is its just and natural ownership; Hungary wants Transylvania back—is it not Hungarian in essence? Most fearsome of all problems, because of the power making its demand, is that of Bessarabia; Russia has never forgotten the loss of that fertile grain province, the more so as the population is very nearly all of Russian origin, no matter where its actual sympathies may lie.

Still further to complicate matters and help Gestapo work along, Transylvania is troubled—or blessed!—with a large German element, composed of the descendants of those pioneers who went wandering in Eastern Europe centuries ago, and never lost their German characteristics when planted among what were to them utterly alien peoples. Then, again, the new Turkey is susceptible to hints (such as von Papen can supply) about her loss of interest in her former Balkan territories, and a redistribution of Roumania's gains would cause her no regrets.

In the immediate post-war years, while Roumania was taking a leading part in the policy and affairs of the Little Entente, her attitude toward Hungary and Germany was such as to store up a good deal of resentment in both countries: to-day there is no Little Entente, but Roumania is, from the Nazi viewpoint, virtually isolated. Fair game, in fact, even if it has to be brought down by foul methods; this last is nothing to the leaders of Nazified Germany.

Gestapo aims in the country were different from those for which the work in Czecho-Slovakia was done, although here, as there, the minorities in the country—and especially the German minority—were used for the accomplishment of those aims. The chief purpose was that of unceasing pressure on the Government, with a view to causing a split between it and France—in effect, to force Roumania to turn to Germany.

To bring this about, all the minorities were wrought upon, reminded of the rights they ought to have as compared with what they had, told of the oppression under which they suffered, and of the insolent injustices perpetrated by the land-owning class. Whether there were truth in the allegations or no mattered not at all: tell an uninstructed peasant that some injustice has been perpetrated in

a village thirty miles away, bring a faked victim of
the alleged injustice to support the story, and insist
that he may be the next victim of something of the
sort—and what will he believe? Fear and sympathy
between them will make of him a malcontent—and
there is another Nazi disciple! Thus the game was
played, and the repercussions of things like these
reached to Bucharest itself. Meanwhile an inces-
sant campaign went on to convince the Central
Government that Germany, and only Germany,
was in a position to check the territorial ambitions
of Hungary, Bulgaria, and Russia. And, after the
break-up of the Little Entente, the complete removal of one of the partners and the immobilization
of the other, Bucharest began to believe. France
had not poured out money like water, had not
formed any organization to sap at Roumanian
institutions and at the same time preach its power
to guard them.

All the while—that is, from 1933 to this present
time, active pressure was maintained through the
open political agitation of the Nazi-supported
Fascist Party known as the Iron Guards, this quite
apart from the indirect, mainly underground and
underhanded activities of the Gestapo. This Fascist
interference in political affairs was far more intense
and effective than the authorities ever allowed to
appear, and the assassination of the Liberal Prime
Minister, Doctor Ion Duca, in 1934, was not only
carried out by the Gestapo, but was openly meant
as a warning to the Government of the lengths to
which Germany was prepared to go. Whether the
reprisals which followed on the assassination of
another statesman this autumn, and the virtual
extinction of open activities by the Iron Guard, will
crush that poisonous organization, cannot yet be

told: German trickery, unscrupulous use of everything between simple lies and bloody murder, and
money without stint, are available to maintain it as
long as any possibility of maintenance exists.

From 1934, by which time the original pair of
workers had bought a nucleus of efficient followers
and trained them intensively in espionage work,
political subversion, and the undermining of their
own country's institutions, Gestapo activities have
been carried on in Transylvania and the Dobrudja,
almost without interference, and controlled from
Bucharest itself and to some extent from Constanza:
a certain amount of camouflage (like that of the
agencies which provided cover for the original pair
of wreckers) has been used, but still more reliance
has been placed on the commodity usually designated as palm oil.

The principal methods used have been those of
instilling fear of danger from the minorities, the
possibilities of obtaining German protection from
that danger by the control of Hungarian and Bulgarian ambitions, and threats of German revenge by
means of the Iron Guard organizations in the event
of any moves being made against Nazi influence: the
average Eastern European of any more than peasant
mentality could appreciate political weapons of this
type, especially when they are used by such skilled
workers as the Gestapo is careful to employ.

German economic penetration of the country has
been much more successful than that by England
and France, because, while the two latter countries
influenced only the Roumanian Government itself
by financial means, and confined themselves to
straight dealing, Gestapo agents used bribes on ın-
dividuals, sought out accessible members of financial
and industrial executives—and of permanent ad-

ministrations as well. There was never any intention of attempting economic sabotage, such as had
been contrived in Czecho-Slovakia: the aim was that
of breaking down and ousting all French and
English economic and commercial interests. Whatever might ultimately be decided as to how Roumania should be treated, whatever part might be
designed for her in Nazi Party plans, the time for
open use of her was and—with the present war
modifying those plans—probably still is regarded as
distant.

Still, possibly as a hint of the influence Germany
could exert, Roumanian currency was subjected to
constant and unexpected pressure by the operations
of the Gestapo-controlled "Black Exchange," which
was easily managed through both Roumanian and
Jewish financial interests. Foreign travellers and
traders in Roumania in the years 1934–8 may
remember how easy it was to clear Roumanian *lei* in
spite of the stringent restrictions in force. There
was a large circle of Bucharest business men, any
one of whom would (and could) arrange for these
"Black Exchange" transactions, which were conducted at a discount of anything between 40 per
cent and 65 per cent. The quantity of Roumanian
currency exported by this means during those years
was very large, and caused continual anxiety to the
Government and the National Bank. Then, even in
such apparently insignificant but in reality highly
important matters as train and air services, by the
time that the Nazi penetration of the country,
backed by Gestapo work, had been thoroughly
organized, the only services that were maintained
with smoothness and punctuality were those connecting Roumania with the Reich, as any traveller
between Bucharest and the West knows.

A survey of all that has been done in Roumania must include some statement of the results of military espionage. It was soon ascertained by Gestapo agents that the frontier defences of the country are neither modern nor powerful, while the equipment of the army is not up to modern standards of mechanization and armament. The plan of operations against Roumania, as worked out by von Fritsch, is aimed not so much at the front lines of defence as at what lies behind them. Internal communications, therefore, were carefully surveyed and mapped, as was done in Poland. Particular attention was paid to all lines of communication with the oilfields of the country, the idea being that the instant destruction of these (the communications, *not* the fields) is absolutely essential as one of the first steps—if not the very first—of a campaign. Thus it would be possible to isolate the fields and their equipment from Roumanian troops, and prevent sabotage until they could be reached and guarded.

Von Fritsch estimated, when the military plans against Czecho-Slovakia were completed, that Prague could be reached from the Reich frontier in twelve hours: he was right. He calculated that the complete overthrow of Poland could be accomplished in three weeks: Russian troops helped in the work at the finish, it is true, but still—von Fritsch was right. A third estimate of his, that by means of German strategy and tactics the Roumanian oilfields can be reached and put under guard within seven days, has not yet been put to the test.

But there is nothing of the slightest military importance between them and the Roumanian western frontier that is not fully marked and described on the maps of the German High Command. The Gestapo has seen to that.

VII

JUGOSLAVIA

IT has been shown that Nazi and Gestapo operations in Roumania, in the absence of any immediacy of action in that country—such as was planned and carried out in Czecho-Slovakia—were directed toward nullifying all French influence and presenting Germany as the only possible agency for the retention of the Dobrudja and Transylvania. The case of Jugoslavia was very different: Goering's intentions regarding it were fully defined, and Gestapo work there was directed to a definite end, in sharp contrast to the opportunism of the Roumanian campaign.

Since the position of Jugoslavia affected the control of the Adriatic and the central part of the Mediterranean, Italy's interests had to be considered; the sphere of influence, or share of the spoils to be awarded to the Fascist Government, was clearly understood between Mussolini and the Nazi leaders. Their combined policy regarding Jugoslavia was pursued quite smoothly and successfully up to a point, but at the very end there appeared an entirely unforeseen and quite impassable obstacle, which prevented the consummation of Italo-German aims and preserved the integrity of Jugoslavia.

German National Socialist policy demanded that the composite State should be treated on lines similar to those followed in Czecho-Slovakia, except

183

that pre-war Serbia was to be retained in a shrunken form as a protectorate of the Reich. The partly German provinces which had formed part of the Austro-Hungarian Empire were to be annexed, giving Germany an initial outlet to the Adriatic and thus to the Mediterranean to the south of the an-nexed province of Austria. This arrangement could, if necessary, be modified in Italy's favour as soon as the Reich either reached or gained indirect control of the Mediterranean coasts of the Balkan penin-sula. Italy was to receive the Croatian and Dalma-tian provinces, together with Albania, joining up through the latter with the German influence which it was—still is—intended to exercise over Greece.

As in Czecho-Slovakia, the work was to be carried through by the use of minorities: Jugoslavia was to be disintegrated by stirring up racial animosities between Croat, Slovene, and German minorities, and the Serbs, and, when things had gone far enough, the Reich would see the necessity of marching in and taking over control to preserve peace. All this was being done, almost to the point of complete success, but intervention on behalf of the minorities had to be stopped at the last minute, because it was realized that the Croats, largest and strongest of the minority races making up the country, would never submit to Italian domination: Mussolini's share of the swag could not be handed to him.

Irrefutable evidence in support of this fact was found in the diplomatic and military records at Vienna after the Anschluss. Antagonism between Italians and Croats (especially on the Croat side) was so intense that it was found necessary during the last war to transfer Croat regiments of the Austrian Army from the Italian front to other points: the Croat soldiers, on more than one occasion, simply went mad at sight of Italian troops, broke up their formations, discarded their rifles, and went for their age-long enemies with no weapons except their knives. Former Austrian officers were found who attested these facts. And Doctor Matchek, the leader of the Croat minority, stated openly that if his people were compelled to call for foreign aid against the Serbs, they would accept that of Germany, but would fight to the death against the Italians.

Neither the combined efforts of Nazis and Fascists, nor the brains of the Gestapo, produced any solution of the problem. If, in any partition of Jugoslavia, Germany had retained the Croat part of the Dalmatian coast, which the Croats would have tolerated as the price of freedom from the Serbs, the great expansionist scheme across the Mediterranean as agreed between Mussolini and the Reich could not proceed. Italy's share of the Mediterranean comprised the central narrows and Algeria, dominated by the island of Pantellaria, and full control of the Adriatic was essential: Germany's allotted place in the plan was farther east. And the deadlock, created over Jugoslavia by this ineradicable hatred between Croats and Italians, found no solution.

But this was not realized either by Italy or the Reich until long after the Gestapo had planted its agents in Jugoslavia, to stir up trouble by means of the minorities to the point that would precipitate German intervention. The original agents were sent, as usual, from the foreign work headquarters in Czecho-Slovakia, and were armed with comprehensive letters of introduction from Henlein and other political minority figures to important German business men in Zaghreb and Belgrade. They carried similar introductions from Slovak political leaders to the heads of the Croat and Slovene minorities. They had also very definite instructions as to the methods of approach to these people, and the extent of the co-operation and help they might promise on behalf of Germany itself. Their strongest safeguard lay in the fact that their activities need not be concealed from the Croat and Slovene leaders, who were not only in sympathy with them, but welcomed their aid, and would help by any means in their power to conceal the aims of these Gestapo workers from the Serb administration of the country.

For full comprehension of the reasons for the effectiveness of Gestapo intervention, a brief statement of the internal affairs of Jugoslavia is essential. At that time, the influence of the Croat political party was becoming very strong. Henlein, with his experience of minority political propaganda in Czecho-Slovakia, had stated his opinion to Smith, then controlling all foreign Gestapo work from his headquarters in Prague: it was to the effect that he saw little hope of aid from the German minority in the Dalmatian provinces, since they were too small in numbers to be effective, though Nazi organizations existed and flourished among them. This coincided with the opinions of both Himmler and Goebbels, and confirmed the impression gathered from the ceaseless foreign investigations of the Gestapo itself.

There were, however, complications of which Henlein knew nothing. One of them was a definite order by Goering, on the Fuehrer's authority, that no Hungarian minority should in any way be involved in internal dissensions—this will be made

clear, together with the reasons for it, in considering Gestapo work in Hungary. The Slovenes were
also few in numbers compared with the Serbs,
although there was no doubt that they would work
with the Croats against the Serbs. To these
Slovenes the Gestapo agents preached ceaselessly
that they must revenge themselves on the Serbs for
what was represented as arrogant exploitation, by
the governing class, of a cultured minority. It was
an almost exact parallel to the situation in Czecho-
Slovakia, where the Sudeten German minority was
taught to regard itself as oppressed by the Czechs.

Until the break-up of the old Austro-Hungarian
Empire, the Croats had been accorded a large
measure of self-determination and control over
their own internal affairs—more, in fact, than the
Czechs had ever been granted by Vienna—while
their close proximity to the Imperial capital had
caused them to absorb and, with more or less
justice, to identify themselves with the culture of
the Austrians. Now they were under the domination of the Serbs, represented to them by Gestapo
agents as no more than a race of peasant farmers,
still tainted by traces of Turkish rule and influence,
and by Mohammedan intolerance, and reserving in
Serb hands just such an exclusive, unyielding
dominance in the Central Government as that of
the Czechs in the conglomerate state across the
Danube. Here was easy propaganda ground for
working, among the biggest minority race of
Jugoslavia.

Thus it was determined that the far smaller
German minority should make no separate moves,
but use its full resources of money and influence to
help the Croats to agitate for separation—and not
only to help, but to urge and further it in every

possible way. This having been arranged, the limit
of German help was offered to Matchek and the
Croat leaders; it was unreservedly accepted, even to
the eventuality of accepting German protection—
anything to break the dominance of the Serbs!
Thus far had Gestapo work inflamed Croat tempers.
Tedious though this recital may have been, it is
important as an example of Gestapo work on purely
political lines. And nothing more was needed,
neither economic sabotage, nor industrial and
military espionage, since military intervention on
any scale involving such additional preparations was
never regarded as necessary: as in the case of the
Czecho-Slovak Republic, it was considered that,
under Gestapo guidance, the differing internal
elements composing Jugoslavia could be set by the
ears until they brought about their own destruction.

The first step taken in conjunction with the
Croat leaders was that of arranging for the selection
of some fifty Croat youths each year, who could be
trained at the Karl University in Prague at the
expense of the Gestapo—which meant that the
Nazi Government would pay. The importance of
this lay in the fact that higher education could only
be obtained in Jugoslavia at the Belgrade University,
or at some subsidiary centre controlled by the
Serbs, and through the medium of the Serb
language. Gestapo agents taught that Serbian was
inferior to either Croat or Slovene tongues, as also
to German, in its application to world culture and
literature: Serbian, it was insisted, was utterly inadequate, and under Gestapo influence and tuition
both Croats and Slovenes flatly refused to learn or
use it, just as the minorities of the Czecho-Slovak
Republic were incited to ignore the Czech language.

By September of 1933, when the academic year
began, the first fifty Croat and Slovene youths were
received in Prague for their enrolment in the Karl
University, for which arrangements had already
been made. They were selected mainly for their
plasticity of mind and reaction to propaganda: their
complete antipathy to Serb control had already
been assured, and this made it easy to show them
the analogy between the position of the Czechs in
Czecho-Slovakia and the Serbs in Jugoslavia, from
which they could deduce as much as they were
taught of the methods needed for their "liberation"
and that of their countrymen.

They were taken in hand by their trained and
enthusiastic fellow-students of the German Sudeten
National Socialist Party and introduced in all the
students' societies and clubs of the Slovak and
Hungarian minorities antagonistic to the Czech
régime. During vacations they were accepted as
guests, through arrangements made by Kuehnel's
Youth Movement in Teplitz-Schönau, in German
and Slovak homes throughout the Republic, and in
every way were educated—soaked might be a better
word for it—into the aims and hopes of National
Socialist policy. They were instructed in the
methods of National Socialist propaganda, and
taken, either individually by German fellow-students with whom they were living, or in collected
parties, to Dresden, only a short journey by road
from Prague by way of Teplitz-Schönau. There they
were shown German culture, the historical associations and points of the ancient city, and were left
to spend week-ends in the Nazi youth sections of
the Dresden Braunhaus, where German youth
could get to work on them.

In particular, in Prague itself they were en-

couraged to mix with youths next due for calling up
for military service, and to hear expressions of disaffection from German, Slovak, Hungarian, and
Ruthenian youths who were compelled as citizens
of Czecho-Slovakia to undergo military training for
the preservation of the Czech régime, which they
had been rigorously taught to despise. Finally, they
were returned to Croatia in time for their own
conscript service, well trained in the technique of
creating disaffection against the Serb majority in the
country.

These contingents of Croat and Slovene students
were received at the Karl University, and financed
by the Gestapo, twice a year, from 1933 to 1937.
The steps thus taken, combined with the methods
already in use by trained Gestapo agents in Jugoslavia itself, assured just such a degree of racial
disintegration of the Jugoslav Army as was achieved
in that of Czecho-Slovakia. By 1937, the army could
not have been effectively mobilized for war, this
quite apart from its insufficiencies of equipment and
material: by 1938, the Serb governing class under
the Romanoff Regent had to face the collapse of the
Little Entente, the fact that for the future no effective help could be expected from France, and complete isolation.

Once given direction by the original Gestapo
agents who entered the country, the political
intrigues of the Croat Party in Jugoslavia needed
nothing more. The party was strong and determined enough to stand on its own feet. Some considerable difficulty was experienced by the Gestapo
in placating or appearing to ignore the aspirations
of the Hungarian minorities, who, naturally, were
not informed of the reasons for ignoring them.
These difficulties became particularly acute after the

Gestapo instigations which led to the assassination
of King Alexander at Marseilles.

The Hungarians were convinced that this was the
German signal for the break-up not only of Jugoslavia, but also that of Roumania, with the consequent return of Transylvania to Hungary. In
point of fact it was nothing of the sort, but was
designed with a view to the destruction of French
influence in Central Europe, and to help in the
complete discrediting of France as an ally.

The cumulative effect on Jugoslavia of such
activities as have been so briefly surveyed may be
judged from the Belgrade Government's reactions
to the successive steps of German policy during the
years under consideration. The Austrian Anschluss, the annexation of Czecho-Slovakia, the occupation of Albania—all these vitally affected the
national existence of Jugoslavia, and the Government at Belgrade did precisely nothing. By the end
of 1938, Jugoslavia was no longer regarded as a
possible ally, even by the most optimistic of democratic prophets. By 1939, the Serbian governing
bloc was offering to make every concession for
which the Croats had asked.

Since a chronological record of these Gestapo
activities throughout Europe, and the necessary
explanations of the Nazi policy which induced
them, is virtually impossible in the scope of such a
survey as this, the countries in which influence on
minorities produced the desired results (Czecho-
Slovakia, Poland, Roumania, and Jugoslavia) have
been grouped for consideration and placed first,
mainly because work outside Germany was begun
in Czecho-Slovakia, and most of the agents used in
that work were recruited from minorities—as were
the Croat students who were financed into the Karl

University. For the rest of Eastern Europe, as for France, England, and the United States, different methods had to be employed: the use of these, and the effects produced by them, can now be surveyed, with no more obtrusion of policy and political moves than is necessary for comprehension of the whole.

VIII

THE EASTERN CORRIDOR

THE broad outline of Nazi policy, as already
indicated, may be defined as a drive to the
Mediterranean, primarily, in three zones: Germany
in the east, Italy in the middle, and a dominated
Spain in the west. It must be understood that the
Nazi and Gestapo operations already described, and
those yet to be described, were and are being conducted simultaneously—at least, as far as the
exigencies and training of personnel for the work
allowed. As regards this last point, the organization and staffing of the Gestapo was pushed on with
feverish speed from 1932 onward, and, directed and
controlled for some time from Czecho-Slovakia as
already stated, had by 1934 been extended to cover
Europe and America in a skeleton form that was
developed and rounded out as has already been
noted in the case of Jugoslavia. With the co-operation of the Italian secret police, the essential parts
of North Africa and the East were also supplied
with agents for the furtherance of German aims,
each man being so trained that he could turn trainer
as soon as he had established himself and made
contact with suitable material.

This survey is concerned now with the German
drive to the south-east, in the first stage of the policy
of world domination already stated; apart from the
countries in which minorities were used to accomplish Gestapo and Nazi ends, there remain the

Balkans, Hungary, and Austria in which German work must be defined, before going on to treat of Western Europe and the wide issues involved beyond it.

The actual annexation of Austria has little to do with the Gestapo: perhaps it might be better to say that the Gestapo had little to do with the annexation, which, as in the cases of Memel and Danzig, was a Nazi Party political matter, which the party machine was fully capable of handling without calling on Himmler or his chief of foreign affairs in Prague. There were no racial minorities to be considered, and there was no need of espionage, either economic or military. It was a case in which political moves only were needed.

Austria was destroyed from within, through political sabotage by its own politicians. In all history, probably, there is no more tragic example of frustrated hopes and helpless futility than the spectacle of the Chancellor, Schuschnigg, paying the final price for his policy of vacillation. By 1937 it had brought Austria to such a position that the Nazi Party, either openly or secretly, controlled practically every branch of Austrian political and economic life.

The Nazi double-crossing policy of threats, bribery, and intimidation by every available means, using Dolfuss against Major Fey, Starhemberg and his Heimwehr organization against them both, while secretly supporting each against the other, and following like tactics in every department of the political administration, had produced complete internal chaos—as, of course, was intended. Neither England nor France gave or could give any effective help. None of the political parties, and least of all the workers and Socialists, had any influence.

Sections of the people, organized or not, would have marched anywhere, had there been anyone to lead them. Those who, like the followers of Fey and Starhemberg, were organized, were used only through their own leaders to double-cross other organizations, and finally, by the machinations of von Papen, to ruin themselves.

Franz von Papen revelled, then as ever, in the maze of intrigue he created, and tangled the web more and more for sheer love of the game. It was he who, having trapped Fey into a desperate personal position, engineered the murder of Dolfuss, which (von Papen must have rubbed his hands with unholy glee) led to Fey's own suicide.

The Gestapo did a little work in Austria, mainly in the field of economic sabotage, with intent to cause pre-occupation on the part of the people with financial losses, and also to destroy the financial interests of London and Paris. The most effective result of their work was the Credit Anstalt crash, which was caused largely by the sabotage of the various insurance corporations which it controlled. Relics of the old Austro-Hungarian Empire, these corporations still operated in Hungary, Czechoslovakia, Jugoslavia, Roumania, and the Reich itself; through their operations they tied up with the Vienna bank and the Austrian Government which supported it with banking institutions in all the countries enumerated here. By financial intrigues and the illegal manipulation of currency and exchange regulations, foreign banks—especially the State Bank of Czecho-Slovakia and the Zivnostvenski Bank of Prague—built up huge claims against the Credit Anstalt. Nazi agents worked unceasingly on foreign holders of large insurance policies of any kind, and ordered all German and Sudeten holders to begin agitation to have their policies surrendered in return for cash compensation. The various political parties of the countries concerned brought pressure to bear on their governments, to compel them to take active measures which would force their national banks to carry out the winding up of policies at surrender values, and to hold up all balances and accruing policy premiums with this end in view.

The central insurance companies in Vienna were thus deprived of all their resources from Central Europe—resources which made up by far the greater part of their revenues—and consequently the Credit Anstalt, and through it the Austrian Government, were forced to throw away huge sums to support the insurance companies. In similar fashion the foreign interests of the Austrian Siemens Electrical Company were sabotaged. Financial chaos not only swallowed up the reserves of the Credit Anstalt, but also wasted the British and French loans, made to Austria, which, instead of helping, merely made the ultimate destruction more certain by holding up the tottering fabric of Austrian finance until the economic structure also collapsed, with devastating effect on the people. And all this was engineered by Gestapo financial experts.

That immediate and decisive action was to be taken against Austria by Hitler was clearly indicated in February of 1937, when the Reichsfuehrer assumed supreme command of the armed forces of the Reich, and Goering dismissed von Blomberg and von Fritsch from their commands. If any doubt had existed, the formation at the same time of the Secret Council of Four—Goering, Goebbels, von Neurath, and von Ribbentrop, and the fact that von Ribbentrop was appointed a member of the Council while still acting as Ambassador in London, should have removed it. Chancellor Schuschnigg was summoned to Germany. He was shown the uselessness of any resistance, and told quite plainly that Austria was to be annexed at once. He was instructed to appoint Goering's nominee, Doctor Seyss-Inquart, as Minister of the Interior. Seyss-Inquart had had his instructions as to what to do: all the internal machinery which controlled public order and the means of resistance was to be set at neutral by him as its political head. The state of confusion and dissension which would inevitably result was to be the excuse for the instant entry of German troops to restore order.

Schuschnigg was further ordered to allay any anxiety which might be felt by England and France over his visit, by announcing that the integrity of Austria had been guaranteed by Hitler. This he did, and to make certainty still more certain he appointed Seyss-Inquart not only Minister of the Interior, but also Minister of Public Safety. Then on March 10th, 1937, ten days after his visit to Hitler, German troops crossed the Bavarian frontier in sight of Hitler's great window at Berchtesgaden, and entered Vienna twelve hours later.

The man who had co-ordinated all the political intrigues with such work as was required of the Gestapo was Baron Franz von Papen, Special Ambassador to Austria. He was responsible for the lies and deceit, the treachery and betrayals, that destroyed Austria, just as he was responsible for the murder of Dolfuss. And that, without going into all the intricate political moves and conflicting personal interests which swayed and influenced the Grand Duchy of the Hapsburgs through all the

post-war years, is all that need be said of Gestapo
work toward the Anschluss.

.   .   .   .   .

Hungary is in a unique position as regards German penetration and Nazification. At about the
time the Gestapo was formed, definite instructions
were issued by Goering, who used Hitler's authority
to back them, to the effect that Hungary was to be
left alone, disregarded, while Hungarian minorities
in other countries were not to be used as was the
case with those of other races.

This is not to say that Gestapo agents were
altogether excluded from Hungary, but they were
planted only to observe and report to Himmler with
a view to completing Gestapo knowledge of Eastern
Europe: what use he made of the reports, he and
Goebbels know; their work is never undertaken
without purpose. Hungary is part of the south-
eastern corridor between Germany and the Mediterranean, and therefore must be known as all else
along the corridor is known.

Still, the use that might be made of Hungary was
one of the things over which Hitler would tolerate
no interference from Goering or anyone else. He
saw the country as bound up with the very essence
of his plans for German world-supremacy, not to
suffer interference by either Goering or by Goebbels
and his propaganda machine. Hitler's initial determination was that of restoring at all costs the former
frontiers of the Reich in the east and south: this, to
his mind, was the indispensable preliminary to the
Nazification of the whole world, and the frontiers
of the Reich as he saw and still sees them are not
merely those of Germany, but of the Austrian
Empire of the Hapsburgs as well. That was in the

beginning of things; he came, before the war of September 1939 began, to see the Reich as a reconstitution of the Holy Roman Empire at the zenith of its power, when, under Charles V it took in Spain and the Low Countries, reduced France to impotence, and made Italy a mere tributary state. All that empire was to be German—his!

Because of Czecho-Slovakia and the men who had made it, the men who worked to keep Austria separate from Germany, and the—to him—intolerable presumption of the Poles in dividing East Prussia from the Reich by a corridor and maintaining Danzig independent of the Reich, his plans were held up. He was determined from the first to re-incorporate Austria and Czecho-Slovakia within his boundaries, and to regain the German provinces of Poland of which Versailles had robbed him. Later, the resistance of the Poles, due to incitement, as he saw it, by England, was regarded by him as a personal affront, and in the frenzy in which he declared that he would "give Poland no light lesson" he determined not merely to take back what he considered German from the Poles, but to destroy them completely as a separate state. It was rather like the God of the Jews issuing an edict of extermination by fire and sword to avenge an insult. And, since the programme suited Goering's book, it was carried through, with the aid from Russia that has been foreseen.

Thus Hungary was considered by Hitler as part of the Greater Germany he would build—but there was a difference between it and the states he destroyed. In the constitution of the old Austrian Empire, it had always ranked as more of an equal partner than any of the other states. The Hapsburgs, on whose great possessions Hitler now looked as his own, had always submitted to the journey to Budapest to receive the iron crown of St. Stephen, while the crown of St. John of Bohemia had never been used since the first Duke of Austria had seized it to make himself an Emperor. If all went well, Hungary would have no future, either geographical or political, except in partnership with Germany, and the allegiance offered to the symbol of Hungarian independence by the Regent Horthy was in reality due to, and offered to, Hitler, guarantor of that independence.

Hungary, then, as Hitler saw it, must wait until her exact place in the jigsaw puzzle of Greater Germany had been prepared to receive her; one thing had to be understood: she must have no intention at any time of entangling herself with anyone else—her destiny was German, and German only. So long as this was comprehended and accepted, neither Hungary nor the minorities outside its borders were to be interfered with. Meanwhile the purely temporary sop of the tiny territory of Ruthenia must be enough for her, although she had, as part of the Austro-Hungarian Empire, held sway over the whole of Slovakia as well.

Thus, as Hitler saw it, and as Goering and the Prussian masters of Germany see it to-day, Hungary stands as no barrier to German progress toward the Eastern Mediterranean, but waits the time when, with the completion of German aims in Eastern Europe, she shall take her place as a partner in, rather than as a tributary to, the Reich. Until that time is ripe, she is to be left alone, say Hitler and Goering.

Bulgaria, flanking the corridor, proved as susceptible to Nazi influence as in fat King Ferdinand's days she was to that of Hohenzollern-governed Germany, and such Gestapo activities as were pur-

sued in that country were for securing confirmation
of existing knowledge, rather than the gaining of
fresh information. The National Socialist Party of
the Reich was convinced from the first that Sofia
would never look farther than Berlin for the fulfil-
ment of Bulgarian aims, and that the real rulers of
the country were prepared to play the part allotted
to them in the campaign of subversion and intrigue,
and war if necessary, designed to further German
expansion. As reward, a nominal Bulgarian independence, at least, could be expected, while total
incorporation in Hitler's Greater Germany would
be the result of resistance.

The broad outlines of Bulgarian policy were, if
not dictated, at least "approved" by Berlin, and
Sofia found it expedient to accept any more or less
vague suggestion that this or that man was eminently
fitted for the post of Foreign Minister, or Chief of
Staff for the Army, exactly as was the case in Hungary. Gestapo agents therefore were confined to a
general sort of surveillance, to make sure that none
of the nominees of Berlin attempted to do any
double-crossing. This work was done with
thoroughness, with almost complete openness, and
with no particular objections being offered by the
Bulgarian authorities.

The chief use of Bulgaria to the Gestapo consisted in the fact that it supplied a very large
number of young men as recruits to its ranks. There
were many reasons why they were particularly
suitable, reasons explained at length in connection
with the training of Gestapo agents. The Bulgarian
contingent, highly trained and completely trusted,
were used for work in many countries, including
the United States, where a group of them were first
to begin the rebuilding of all that von Papen had

destroyed in 1917—and more. The organization constructed in the States for Gestapo use is far more powerful and dangerous than that of which von Papen was head until he "forgot" his portfolio on the way to New York with the rest of the German ambassadorial staff.

To complete the preparations for the establishment of a south-eastern corridor through the Balkans when German plans in other directions had been sufficiently advanced, a close watch, economic and political, had to be kept on Greece and Turkey. The principal moves were political: Germany had to create and foster in every way a belief in both those countries that their future interests could only be served by co-operation with the Reich. Pro-German sympathies had always existed in both countries; nothing must be admitted that might decrease, let alone change, those sympathies. On the contrary, the swift rise of German influence together with the decline of that of France in South-eastern Europe, the insistence on Italian claims in the Mediterranean, must be preached and published and used to increase belief in Germany as the world-power of to-morrow.

With all this, a vague theory was put about by means of Gestapo political burrowers that the future of South-east European commerce would be best assured, not by way of the Mediterranean, but through use of the natural channel of the Danube to the Black Sea. Russia, with its vast population and enormous potentialities for both production and consumption, would play a main part in the use of the Danubian avenue, and, favourable to if not actually allied with Germany, would assure prosperity to both Greece and Turkey. In some such fashion the theory was put about.

The vast expansionist aims of Germany were explained to these two countries with tempting modifications, and in ways that presented their accomplishment as an utter inevitability. Opposition to Germany, it was shown, would mean war, and the possibility of France and England being able to render aid against the might of the Reich was an absurdity: this doctrine was—still is—sedulously preached, and no French nor English organization exists in either country to controvert it.

The need for military espionage is non-existent, either in Bulgaria, Greece, or Turkey. In this last-named country, the German High Command had assumed complete control of all armed forces during the last war, and the country was mapped in detail in German records. Some observation was kept on new modifications and was made simple by the fact that Germany quickly worked a way into the economic developments of both Greece and Turkey so that no financial allocations could be made for any purpose, military or otherwise, without Berlin knowing it. Then, to deal with any difficult or unforeseen circumstances that might present themselves, the ingenious diplomat and accomplished spy, von Papen, after completing his mission of destruction in Austria, was dispatched to Stamboul as Ambassador to Turkey.

With his very able and utterly unscrupulous assistance, there was little possibility of the National Socialist policy being thwarted or failing to produce the desired effects. The only danger was that of von Papen's yielding to his lust for intrigue to such an extent as to disrupt the Turkish Government and bring premature trouble on the country, out of sheer exuberance. But, since his work in Austria, he had been permitted to act only at the instigation of special Gestapo agents, and Himmler in Berlin, von Papen's master, now, was coldly watchful of him and of all that he did.

That he carried out his instructions ably is evident from the trend of Turkish foreign policy in 1938, and still more so in 1939. The way of the south-eastern corridor is planned, all but prepared; beyond it lie Egypt, all of Africa, India, all of Asia up to the point where Japan must be granted a share in the spoils. If . . .

IX

WESTERN EUROPE AND SCANDINAVIA

THE operations of the Gestapo in Western Europe, though of a different nature from those already described, are easily comprehended if the broad outlines of Germany's aims at expansion, already stated, are remembered. Work in the West kept pace with the development of Nazi Party political energies, these latter governed by Hitler's utter conviction that all his aims could be achieved without war, though at the same time provision was made for the alternative eventuality. Goering and the Prussian element in the movement, ultimately to become its masters, knew from the outset that war must result, but they made no effort at impressing the fact on Hitler's mind, lest in so doing they should modify his aims: Prussianism *is* war: let him go on in the belief that there would be no war; they knew, and were content.

Yet, as both Hitler and Goering, and his party saw it, if the elimination of France as a first-class power, and the isolation of England, could be achieved, then whatever military resistance might be made by either—or of both, for that matter—would not be serious enough to affect Nazi aims. For— and here the limitation of the German and especially of the Prussian mind, its inability to get the points of view of other peoples, becomes apparent—with France weakened and Britain isolated, Holland and Belgium would automatically become German protectorates, while Switzerland could be divided up between Germany and Italy. South Africa would already have become a German outpost, Canada would have allied itself to the United States, while Australia would have been handed over to Japan, and any steps isolated and crippled England might take would be utterly useless, any "war" a mere farce. Fantastic though all this may seem to non-German, Western minds, it is a reality and impelling force with Adolf Hitler. The world, Nazified, is to be his.

This conception, on which work in Western Europe was based from the outset, does not mean that military espionage was neglected, but that the chief aim to which Gestapo energies were devoted was economic surveillance, especially on any tie-up between France and Belgium. Both Belgium and Holland were used, from the beginning of work in the West, as bases for Gestapo supervision and penetration. This applies more particularly to Belgium. Brussels was chosen as the most suitable liaison point between the Cologne headquarters on the one hand, and Western Europe and America on the other. Amsterdam became the meeting-place for all actual contacts between German and foreign agents in cases where it would have been inadvisable to receive the foreigners in Germany itself. In this latter connection, it may be remembered that in more than one recent British espionage trial evidence has been produced to show that, in the course of his work, the spy went to or held communications with Amsterdam: usually he went there, one or more times.

Both these points were selected for a number of reasons, in addition to their geographical positions. Amsterdam is the one city of Holland which can be described as quite cosmopolitan in character, largely by reason of the diamond trade, the constant stream of visitors that it brings, and the multitude of business and personal interminglings that it causes. German agents and their non-German co-workers would have little difficulty in avoiding notice among so mixed and floating a population. In particular, important German officials of the Cologne Gestapo control could easily keep themselves anonymous and unrecognized in the city, while meeting agents whom it would be inadvisable to bring into Germany itself. Communications in either direction, either by rail or road, are easy and quick, and the similarity of the German and Dutch languages is another factor in inconspicuousness.

The advantages of Belgium for a wider form of activity are equally pronounced. There is a considerable amount of internal bickering between the Walloon and Fleming sections of the people, of which, without working on "minority" lines, advantage may be taken; the anxiety of the Government to preserve neutrality on all sides gives judicious foreigners some amount of immunity from official supervision; the country is easily accessible from all sides, and from the sea. It was also, until recently, possible to cross the frontiers on three sides—into Holland, France, or Luxembourg—without passports, identity cards or driving licences being sufficient, while on night trains supervision was so lax that even these proofs of identity were not always necessary. A week-end ticket was enough to secure entry to England.

Thus the main pre-occupation of the Gestapo was that of assuring the anonymity of agents and couriers, and high German officials making contact from Cologne, who would be continually entering and leaving both Holland and Belgium. Everything in the internal constitutions of the two countries was favourable to this end, and, as an additional safety factor, the principal railway communications of Europe proved so well adapted that they might have been designed with Gestapo needs in mind.

Entry could be obtained either to Belgium or Holland from France, Luxembourg, or Germany, while by juggling with trains it was possible, if need arose, for a traveller to show that he had arrived from practically any country or direction, east, west, or south. As instance: a through express train service was instituted from Vienna to London, with continental terminals at Flushing and Ostend. It was timed to connect at Vienna with express services from Italy, which in turn connected with France from Budapest and the Balkans; there were also connections with the Orient expresses, both west-bound and east-bound; with the expresses of the southern route from Madrid and Lisbon to Stamboul, and vice versa. At Nuremberg in Germany, this Vienna–London express was timed to connect with the Orient expresses, east- and west-bound, of the northern route, which entered Germany from France at Strasbourg and so ran east to Prague and Bucharest with branches at Brno to Berlin, Warsaw, and Moscow; also with the daily express Blue Train from Prague to Paris.

The Nuremberg connection was timed for two a.m., so that a passenger from the east- or west-bound trains could change at that most quiet hour, almost certainly free of interested observation, to the waiting north-bound. Thence the train passed through Cologne, to break into two parts at the frontier; one part was for Amsterdam and Flushing, the other for Brussels and Ostend. It was completely impossible to ascertain either the starting-point or even the general direction from which any passenger on the train might have come, unless he chose to reveal and prove it.

In selecting and dealing with Holland and Belgium, the Gestapo chiefs took into consideration that, if war in the West became inevitable, the neutrality of both countries was at Germany's discretion; if they remained neutral, they would be bases for espionage not only in Western Europe, but on the sea too. Preparations, made to meet this eventuality, involved a new and carefully considered technique which, as it was applied also to Scandinavia, and for a modified purpose also to France and England, merits full description later.

Gestapo activities in Switzerland were largely directed to close surveillance of political personages visiting Geneva; political aims in connection with the Federal Government were in the hands of the local Nazi parties in the German and Italian cantons, assisted as these were by the parent party machine. The observation kept on statesmen visiting the League of Nations was very thorough; the terrain could not have been more suitable for Gestapo purposes if the League had chosen its home with those purposes in mind. It was particularly unfortunate for the Government of Czecho-Slovakia that its couriers to and from Geneva had so often to pass through German territory and the railway junction at Nuremberg. On many occasions they were deliberately and purposely held up by juggling with trains and special coaches, so that opportunity was made for examination of their attaché cases and portfolios. The same measures were taken at Turin

and Vienna, in the event of journeys by the
southern route through Italy and Austria.

·   ·   ·   ·   ·

In France, the work of the Gestapo was based on
a number of points that governed or affected Nazi
policy. Foremost of these was Hitler's determination to exact revenge for France's part in the war of
1914–18 and for her share in framing the Treaty of
Versailles: not in the way that he would be
revenged on Austria, Czecho-Slovakia, and Poland,
but by the humiliation of France to the status of a
second-class power, without allies, as has already
been stated. Hitler's view was that France pursued
a policy of stringent, bitter repression against
Germany, a policy dictated by fear; he planned to
use that same fear against France herself, to work
for internal disruption and a cleavage between
France and England, so that the Republic would
stand utterly alone.

The first objectives were economic and political;
military espionage was also necessary, but in the
technique to be employed it was to be combined
with industrial espionage in such a way that it would
endure and be effective even in the eventuality of
war, not only up to the outbreak of hostilities, but
also beyond that point.

All this called for most careful and patient preparations, which would take time to complete. It
would require, too, very carefully trained men, and
these had to be selected and taught their work
beyond the possibility of error. The work fell
naturally into three stages: first, the training of the
operating agents; then, their penetration into the
economic and political life of France and, more
important still, into the social life of the French

people; thirdly, through their social contacts, to secure the means of continuance of industrial and military espionage and sabotage after the outbreak of war, even though the agents themselves might no longer be on French soil. This ultimate aim, continuance of the work under all circumstances, applied to Western Europe generally, to the Scandinavian countries, and to the U.S.A. as well. It was very simply planned, with the realization that in anything involving the employment of a body of operatives, success is dependent on simplicity of method. Since it was the final stage of the Gestapo's work, the other two must first be detailed.

Agents were selected and trained, mainly in the Sudetenland of Czecho-Slovakia, the principal training-ground for all Gestapo workers designed for use outside Germany. They were not of German nationality, for Smith, Himmler's chief aide in foreign work, had forced on both Himmler and Goebbels, and on Goering too, understanding of the fact that the German mentality is completely unable to detach itself from national considerations and so does not lend itself to objective survey of any problem. The doubtful value of all German agents is due to this fact—they see everything through German spectacles, with German prejudices, and thus miscalculate reactions other than German.

Great care was taken over the selection of these agents: main essentials were cosmopolitan tendencies, a detached and objective viewpoint and independence of nationalism, ability to absorb atmosphere in training outside their own countries, total disregard of all codes of ethics so far as their work was concerned, suave and charming manners, strength of character and personality combined with utter lack of what is commonly known as conscience. This last was an especial requisite, since the men chosen would be set to tasks that they could not justify to themselves as bona fide secret service work for their own country: there were, for instance, Frenchmen among them set to work against France, and Englishmen against England. Both the Sureté in Paris and the Special Branch in England know whether they were effective or not.

It may be remembered that at the conference in Munich, at which the Gestapo was formed, Himmler had asked where such men were to be found, and had been told—"We shall not find them: we shall create them." Such men *were* found and trained—created, in fact—for the purposes for which they were required.

They began their operations in France at two points, Lyons and Roubaix. In the former city, three of them were enrolled at the Ecole Superieure de Commerce, where they would continue for two years, and one was entered in the service of a silk manufacturer of the district: only two were sent to Roubaix. They consisted of three Sudeten-German youths with Czech admixture in their origins, a Slovak youth whose father had been Roumanian, a Hungarian whose parents had been forced to change their nationality from mixed Austro-Hungarian to Czech by the peace treaties, and a young Croat of partly Italian origin from Ragusa. Any one of them could have mixed and held his own in a gathering of any European nationality, and passed as a citizen of more than one country other than his own.

There were sound reasons for choosing Lyons as

a centre from which to begin Gestapo operations. It is a French provincial city, to all intents, but in the aspects which the Gestapo sought and needed, it is more cosmopolitan than the average Englishman or American can realize. It is on the main Paris–Marseilles railway route, and its railway station, the Gare de Perrache, is a long "halt" for connections with the west and with Switzerland in the east, Geneva being only one hour distant. The "halt" is therefore for all passengers travelling between North Africa and the South of France, and Paris, Switzerland, and of course Belgium and England as well. It is on the confluence of two great rivers, the Rhone and Saone, both connected by great waterways with Paris and Strasbourg. It is almost on the fringe of the great fortifications of Bellagarde, the point at which, from the Swiss frontier, the Maginot Line might be turned. It is a great military training centre, with soldiers and young officers always in evidence. It is the centre of one of France's chief industries, that of silk manufacture, and contains a large number of wealthy and influential business-men.

Its politics, through Herriot, are largely Socialist, and it contains the most truly democratic university in Europe, to which come students from almost every European country, and from the French and Spanish North-African colonies. In addition, one at least of the heads of the Gestapo knew the city intimately, and had social connections among its business-men, university professors, and students.

All these advantages had been taken into consideration when, at Munich, the system of Gestapo operations had first been planned, and the turning down of Captain Roehm's own suggestions had given the Chief of Staff his first inkling that the

leadership of the secret police was not destined to
be awarded to him. At that time, too, the *modus
operandi* of work outside Germany had been
planned, and for some eighteen months after, the
young men who were to lead the way into espionage
in France had been under intensive training in the
Sudetenland.

By the end of 1933 they were considered fit to
begin their tasks; by the beginning of 1934 they
were all installed in the posts which had been
prepared in advance for their occupation, all of
them entering France with Czech passports. Those
who were enrolled in the Lyons School of Commerce entered it on the personal recommendation
of one of its professors, and both he and the young
member of the silk manufacturing firm who received
the fourth into his business acted in complete
ignorance, solely with the friendly wish to oblige
the head of Gestapo external work, whom they
knew in quite a different and harmless capacity.

The operations which were to be initiated from
Roubaix had an equally simple "planting." The
head of a large manufacturing concern, with
branches throughout northern industrial France,
was also a personal friend of the chief of Gestapo
external affairs, whom he, too, knew only as a professional man of purely academic interests. He
readily agreed to find openings for a couple of
highly trained and smart young men recommended
by such a one, and was both willing and able to
arrange all the formalities necessary for their
residence in France and work in his establishment
on the commercial side—which, of course, involved
travelling between his headquarters and branch
establishments.

Thus the first Gestapo agents were introduced to

France. The aims of all of them were similar, but those working from Lyons, having greater advantages, were given a wider scope than their associates in Roubaix, who concentrated mainly on the great industrial areas of north-eastern France—the cockpit of the last war's opening stages. They would all work very slowly and carefully—so much so, in fact, that the first year or so could only be regarded as a final stage of the training they had already received.

They did not regard themselves as agents whose urgent duty it was to begin spying in order to provide copious and detailed reports on the French Army, nor did they expect to proceed at once to the Quai d'Orsay and obtain a copy of the secret treaty which was to be handed to the glamorous blonde waiting in a compartment of the Orient express. The Gestapo was prepared to wait until the Government of the Reich was less pre-occupied with internal affairs, and the first task confronting these operatives was comparatively simple—that is simple to them. It was merely that of making friends, and taking care to choose friends whom they could use.

In making friends they had little or no difficulty, being presentable, apparently ingenuous, perfectly mannered, attractive and athletic young men; they had only to meet people, and multitudes of opportunities faced them. As for using such friends as they might make, they were entirely conscienceless —coldly ruthless, in fact—and a very large part of the training given them had been directed to this end, fitting them for every type of social contact, and using it to their own advantage and that of the Gestapo.

The Lyons section had choice among three thousand or so students from every part of France and Spain and the colonies, and all the student café

and club intimacy in which to choose acquaintance-
ships and deepen them to more than mere acquaintance. As foreign students, not returning to their
own countries during vacations, they could accept
invitations which would bring them into touch with
French family life of many grades; where their personal qualities made them acceptable, they could
get into the lives and social activities of families,
play on the susceptibilities of women, and so bur-
row a way into the real, intimate life and relation-
ships of the circles to which they were admitted.
"Le sport" was a great factor; athleticism is a passport to many social circles, and they were all
capable of using it to the full. Then, again—this
particularly in respect of the pair located in Roubaix
—their intelligence and cosmopolitan breadth of
outlook, combined with command of languages,
gave them a footing among business-men far older
than themselves, and invited confidences which led
to friendships. Equally true of the Lyons group,
these qualities combined with political knowledge
and ability in debate made them popular and even
leaders in student societies.

In student vacations and on business missions,
these wolves in sheep's clothing travelled virtually
all over France in the course of a year or two, and as
they travelled they observed, inferred, and deduced,
trained as they were to observe everything, forget
nothing, weigh the relative values of all details.
Chosen in the first place because they possessed
these abilities, they had been trained to develop and
use them to the full, and taught the consequences
of error. Unsuspected as they were—and never was
one of the group suspected of being other than he
appeared—they could retrieve such errors as they
made, and profit by them.

Thus they tabulated and recorded everything as time went on. Names and professions—an unbelievably formidable list of these went to Himmler's archives—lives and ambitions, money and the lack of it, rich youths who might prove pliable, and poor ones who had strength of character or might be open to bribery, business-men who put self-interest before national well-being, politicians to whom power was more than straight dealing, and members of the official classes who might be accessible, or on the other hand might be dangerous. In the students' cafés they met elder brothers, men who had finished with student life and begun the world, and who returned for a glimpse of the old life in which they discussed their own professions and interests with the freedom that came of being among their own kind.

Very valuable from the Gestapo standpoint, too, were students who, called up for military service, returned on long or short leave to their old haunts, and chattered with their friends about the army and navy and air force—about the chasseurs, the artillery, or the Spahis; about the wonderful improvements that had been made in the ".75," the new anti-tank gun of an effectiveness incredible, capable of piercing this or that thickness of armour-plating; the fortification at X, with a thickness of concrete more formidable than that at Y, and of the elevator which, with a speed incredible, would take you down a hundred and twenty feet to the galleries of the underground works—and so on, interminably.

Former students revisiting the cafés and hailing from Algiers, Tunis, or Morocco, would remark on troops here and warships there; would tell of political moves as they saw them, of native unrest, of the efficiency or futility of colonial officials, and intimate details of commercial and industrial interest which nobody but the younger members of families engaged in great concerns could know—youngsters so completely trusted that the possibility of their innocently making such revelations was ignored by their elders. All these things would be remembered, sifted, checked with parallel revelations, and recorded. It was all so very simple—terribly, tragically simple.

One of those Lyons café centres for students, perhaps the most important of them all, merits special mention, since an idea of the facilities it offered conduces to clear understanding of the success with which these young, initial Gestapo agents carried out their orders. It was and still is in the Place de la Republique in Lyons, and occupies the cellars of a large tenement house, underlying the whole block of building and consisting of a veritable maze of arched and buttressed cellars, all communicating with each other, either directly or by means of low-ceilinged connecting passages, along which last exist smaller cellars used as wine stores, larders, and the like, and so great is the simple trust reposed by the patron in his clientele, mostly open and unguarded. A big, arching-roofed main cellar serves as bar, with the usual zinc-covered counter on one side, trestle tables and wooden benches all round the walls and in the alcoves, and the centre space full at any hour of students arguing, drinking, introducing everyone to everyone else, singing or dancing.

The café begins its day at eight in the morning, when it is thronged with students hurrying in for bowls of coffee and croissants as sustenance on which to support themselves during the first lectures of the day. From that time, until two or three o'clock of the next morning, the place is full, and no matter how much of music, shouting, singing or horse-play disturbs the Place outside, sometimes even up to dawn itself, no gendarme does more than push his head into view from the top of the steps to voice a conciliatory protest, on which he is subjected to a fire of good-humoured banter by everyone near enough to the staircase for sight of him, and finally beckoned down by the patron to be presented with a large glass of *fin du maison*, a cognac worth knowing, and dispensed from the "stock bottle," which holds about two gallons.

Into such an atmosphere the Gestapo young men entered, to be made free of the place, welcomed, and treated as good fellows. It should be fairly easy to realize that, trained observers and indefatigable workers as they were, they had an immense knowledge of France and the French people after the lapse of two years—that is, by the end of 1935, when the Gestapo chiefs were beginning to see results from their work in Eastern Europe, and were ready to receive and co-ordinate reports from the west, and to direct the second stage of the work there.

The young men who had been entered to work at Roubaix had not been idle; their activities had been directed to a more specialized end, that of obtaining detailed information of the heavy industries, including positions of factories, reserve stocks of material available, output, capacity for increase of output, transport, communications, railway junctions and sidings, qualities and types of machinery in use, staffs, employed, possibilities of causing unrest, and other points from which a complete knowledge of industrial France might be gained. In addition, they had used all possible efforts toward making a wide circle of friends among youths of their own age or thereabouts, choosing those who, from the circumstances of their lives and families, would become skilled workers in these virtually key industries. This was of the utmost importance, as the workers thus contacted and rendered accessible complemented the students of engineering, science, and chemistry faculties similarly listed by the Gestapo men at Lyons, and marked as future technical and executive heads in establishments in which the Roubaix victims would be employed. Apart though they were, the two sections worked in unison.

Thus two of the three stages previously noted as necessary for the full working of Gestapo penetration of France were completed by September of 1935, and the time had come to begin the third stage, that of assuring the continuity of the work during war, and even in the absence of these highly trained and fully efficient agents. There were other branches of work to be done as well, and it may be advisable to trace, in brief outline, the course which Gestapo activities as a whole took during the next few years, and at least indicate a few of the things for which the organization was responsible, directly or indirectly.

Between 1934 and 1938, the Gestapo operatives in France were directly behind and responsible for much of the industrial unrest which caused such internal economic confusion, and resulted in the political upheavals which limited the lives of so many successive governments to a few months—or even weeks. They were behind the greater part of the financial scandals, such as the Stavisky affair, which was organized with the help of members of the forgotten financial fraud organization of

Madame Hainalt and the *Gazette Française* of 1930. This last was designed for a purpose and betrayed for a purpose, and, born in the dingy municipal pawnshop of Bayonne, as was consonant with the Gestapo technique, shook the confidence of the French people and of financial authorities in the Central Government, time after time. It was the means by which French financial relations with their Central European allies were discovered, and invariably the discoveries were used by Germany to cause financial confusion both for France and her allies.

Gestapo agents discovered the financial interests through which the Jewish-controlled banks of Germany and Central Europe were operating, and their methods of operation, and then severed the connections between them and France. They penetrated deeply into every department of the economic and industrial life of the country and made exhaustive reports to Himmler's bureaux. A Gestapo inquiry from the Control for almost any kind of information was swiftly answered—even such specialized inquiries as the extent of the co-operation between French and English interests in the technical processes for boring gun barrels.

In the matter of military espionage, the technique of von Fritsch was followed. Frontier defences were regarded as relatively unimportant for the time, but the interior of the country was divided into sections or zones, each allotted to a specially trained man who, working on existing large-scale maps, made certain that every road, railway, junction, siding, bridge, factory, power station—everything that could possibly be of direct or indirect military importance—was clearly and accurately marked, as had been done in Poland.

Details affecting the extent of military establishments and training were also considered unimportant, or as of only minor importance, since the
von Fritsch scheme relies on observation from the
air for knowledge of troop movements and concentrations at and behind the front. A vast mass
of accurate information concerning defences and
materiel was gathered, bit by bit, in the course of the
years over which the work extended. As an illustration: young men of successive years of military
service, but called up to serve in the same military
zone in those successive years, had provided not
only a check on information given by the class
called in the first of those years, but had let slip also
—quite in ignorance of the damage they were doing,
of course—the nature of any improvements or
alterations in armaments and equipment. All this
was noted and tabulated for use of the German
High Command. This applied not only to France
itself, but also to the French colonies, and to those
of North Africa in particular.

Gestapo workers made a special study of French
Intelligence, and gained an extensive knowledge of
the working of the Second Bureau, its personnel,
and even its particular activities at a given time. One
of these agents, in particular, appeared to be completely at home in the big building in the 17th
arrondisement of Paris which housed the staff of
the *Etat Major*. In this connection it should not
be forgotten that the friendships contracted in
students days at Lyons and elsewhere were never
allowed to lapse, but followed up with much
warmth and persistence—such as were likely to
prove useful, at least—for long afterward. For
instance, through the period of military service.
Thus, in the course of a few years, those initial

Gestapo workers could count among their friends army and naval officers, doctors in the services, and men in every branch of politics, commerce, shipping, and industry. These friendships were backed by the open confidence and trust of student days together, and the Gestapo youths as students had made themselves popular, had been socially known and recommended—their positions were unassailable, and all who had known them considered them worthy of trust. And all these friendships were *used*, as only such men, specially selected and trained for work of the sort by that devil's own college, the Gestapo, could use them.

They had begun by making themselves *persona grata* in students' clubs. Now, apparently launched on careers, young men of substance, they met and knew and dealt with politicians, bankers, directors, trustees, mayors of cities, and on the other hand with trade unions officials, workers, merchant sailors, and the underworld figures of cities. They were quite at home, accepted without question on the credentials they were able to present and the introductions they could furnish from unimpeachable sources, in the Club Royale, the Bal Tabarin, a workmen's café in Clichy, the Palais du Peuple, or the Salvation Army hulk on the Seine. They were responsible for deflections of the forces of both capital and labour, and directed the repercussions to the undermining of political and economic stability.

They controlled such special workers as were sent to engage in the forms of military espionage that were regarded as necessary, and the Nazi—as distinct from the Gestapo itself—agents in industrial and commercial quarters. These latter were the second line of attack; the Gestapo men, fully settled in France, were the governors, acting singly as over-seers, directors, and at no time were there more than eight of them in the country, for trained specialists of the sort were not easy to find and fit for their tasks, and lesser men could do the spade work. They were fully trusted in every way. Seldom were their communications with headquarters committed to paper, and it may be said, in a general way, that they were so well trained as to need neither notes nor plans which might have betrayed their real purpose in the country. They passed information on to "contacts" met casually in the street or in a hotel lounge, or whom they might meet in a quite open motor-trip to Ostend or Brussels, or a ski-ing expedition to Switzerland in the course of which they would pass through Geneva. They carried no papers which might identify them with the Gestapo, but had simple and reliable means of identifying themselves to their "contacts," and of assuring themselves of making contact with the right persons.

The most difficult task these men—for by the time they came to the task the students and youngsters of the first days had become responsible men—had to accomplish was that of selecting and infecting a number of youths belonging to the country in which they were working (this applies not only to France, but to England and the Scandinavian countries as well) with their own doctrines and aims, and making certain that these victims would follow blindly and unquestioningly along the ways indicated to them. This was no easy task, even after likely subjects had been found: it was not enough to work on vanity, ambition, dissatisfaction, or any single factor in particular, nor to buy a youngster with money or the promise of desperate adventure such as appeals to youth. One or more of these attributes might indicate a likely disciple, but there must also be the germ of emotional urge, a quality more easily recognized than described as part of the make-up of an individual. Such a one, when found, had to be so worked on that he accepted the views drummed into him, saw only through the eyes of these men and only what they wanted him to see.

To explain how all this was accomplished would be as tedious as a psychological treatise. There are, in every society, rebels against constituted authority who will go to any lengths to disrupt it, and among these may be found intellectual abilities of very high order, together with courage and pertinacity—and these exist in every stratum of society. The trained, passionless, and utterly unscrupulous Gestapo agents chose such persons, taking only the young and plastic, and worked on them, made what was wanted of them, one here and one there. Not a great number were needed, but they must be so carefully chosen that each one, like his mentor, would be capable of accomplishing a great deal.

One of them might occupy the position of a skilled worker in, say, the rolled sheet metal industry; of him would be required enough information to cover all the details of that industry in the area in which he was employed—or, at least, to draw reliable inferences on the extent, progress, and capacities of the industry. As an example of this: the speed of an aeroplane is dependent, among many other factors, on the resistance to heat of the metal used for construction of the engine exhaust: if all factors, with the exception of the exhaust pipes, gave a very high rate of speed, then such speed could not be attained until an alloy had been found which would stand up to the terrific heat of the exhaust. A metal worker, hearing that experiments were being made with a view to producing such an alloy, one with a heat resistance greater than that of anything of which he had knowledge, would give the necessary clue, which would be followed through connecting links in the various sections concerned with aeroplane engine design, technical and experimental, until the composition of the new alloy was revealed and passed on through Himmler's headquarters to German technicians.

It has already been noted that the Gestapo men at Lyons made the contact with executive and controlling side of industries, while those at Roubaix were more concerned with finding suitable material on which to work among the labour elements. Both were equally necessary, and, it may be said, enough of the required material was found. These actual spies on their own country worked for the Gestapo for many reasons, and in most cases a perverted idealism, carefully divorced from nationalism by their mentors, was a large if not the chief factor. It was considered utterly impossible that any of them should be detected, though at times that calculation proved erroneous, since both in France and England some few of them were detected and their activities nullified before the outbreak of war. For the most part, they were careful to avoid any traceable acquaintance with or even knowledge of foreigners, or interest in subversive elements among their own people. Most of them had families and friends, life-long connections in the districts to which they belonged, and could be vouched for by local notabilities and authorities.

With the selection, enlistment, and training of these—social perverts, they may be termed—the third part of the programme for Western Europe, as worked out at Munich in the beginning of Gestapo organization, was completed. Not that work ended at that point: it went on, goes on yet, and will go on as long as there is a Nazi Party with a Gestapo to enforce its doctrine by any form of treachery, oppression, or violation of accepted principle that may seem useful.

In all these activities, women and feminine influence have been ignored. As will be seen in connection with the training of Gestapo agents, the avoidance of all feminine influences was a cardinal point, due to the simple hypothesis that a woman will work only for one man, and then only if that man works for her and for no other. It was also stressed that a woman will work only at the dictates of her emotions, and not for ideals, and above all is incapable of pursuing understandingly and objectively a single purpose to its logical end.

That is not to say that Gestapo agents are sexless —far from it. They have used and still use women to gain their own ends, and work on them through their emotions when necessary, but always with calculation for effect, and with the cold ruthlessness inculcated during training. A woman to them is something to use, and even play with as long as she is of use: after that, she is to be discarded, shown that she is no longer wanted—and, above all, she is never to be trusted in any way that could affect the work of the man who has used her. At times, the female spy, glamorous or otherwise, had her place in the system inaugurated by Stieber—the story of Mademoiselle Lison, already related, goes to prove this. But in the composition of the Gestapo she has no place whatever: she simply does not exist.

The foregoing outline indicates how industry was penetrated by the Gestapo, but it was not in that department of activity alone that work was done. Agents of like nature were found, proselytized, and trained for analogous work in commerce, in government departments, in banking establishments, and particularly in shipping companies. These last received special attention, since, in the event of war, the movements of the whole mercantile marine of the world would be—as now they are—of vital interest to Germany. Failing knowledge in advance of such movements, a submarine campaign would lose half its effectiveness, and results obtained in connection with the shipping of neutral countries toward the end of the first month of war go to show that the information was forthcoming—the Gestapo was doing its work.

In the neutral countries of the West, Belgium, Holland, and the Scandinavian group, Gestapo work followed the lines of that carried on in France, though with less intensity. The chief aim was that of establishing a system of espionage, political and military up to a point, but mainly economic with special attention to communications, which meant shipping. This was done in a much easier way than could be found for work in France, and, as so often proved the case, the means to the desired end were found in Czecho-Slovakia.

Commercial houses of purely Czech composition in Bohemia abolished the German language completely in favour of the resuscitated Czech, when the industries got going under republican rule; they insisted on the use of the Czech language and nothing else, in the conduct of their businesses. This, since the language was inadequate in some ways for business purposes, caused confusion enough in their own internal economy; especially was this the case when it came to records and books of account. As a medium for foreign correspondence, the language was hopelessly impossible, so much so that something had to be done about it. The Czechs would not solve the difficulty by using German, which they all understood quite well, and, since their export trade with the Low Countries and Scandinavia developed to highly profitable dimensions, young employees were interchanged with those countries, both in the offices for correspondence and in the works to gain knowledge of interchangeable technical terms. This applied even to such an agricultural country as Denmark, since Czecho-Slovakia exported quantities of its subsidized beet sugar to that country, receiving in return foodstuffs, especially barrelled and pickled pork, which would not have been accepted from Germany even if adequate supplies could have been obtained from that country.

In consequence of all this, there were in Prague, Pilsen, Brun, Bratislava, and other large towns, numbers of young clerks and technical and mechanical workers of Scandinavian, Danish, Belgian, and Dutch nationalities, all speaking languages more or less similar to German, and in blood, at least, much closer to the Germans than to the Slavonic Czechs. Thus, alien and perhaps a little unhappy as these youngsters were in the strange environment and among the unfamiliar, almost ununderstandable people of Czecho-Slovakia (who never spoke German if they could avoid it) it was a very simple matter for the Gestapo, with Nazi Party help, to "adopt" these young men on various pretexts, and "adapt" any of them who were suitable and willing to fill the positions in which it was intended to place them when they returned to their own countries.

They were politically educated on Nazi lines, and also were materially and financially helped when opportunities presented themselves. Their paths in this strange country were made smooth and easy; the youth organizations adopted them, nursed them politically, and infused into them by example as much as by precept enthusiasm for the glorious principles of National Socialism, through which a whole new world would eventually be evolved. All the methods which had been so thoroughly perfected in dealing with German youth were applied, and in such of the foreigners as were completely converted and passed as reliable, the Gestapo found the tools it needed.

They went back to their own countries, each with a large bonus ostensibly given by their Czech employers, and distributed themselves as required—and directed—in key industries, particularly in those of shipping, transport, cable and wireless, and in fact every sort of communications. Naturally, it was almost impossible to detect whether they were or were not engaged in espionage, and as, in the event of war, they would be working in neutral countries, the strain on such consciences as they had left was not enough to prevent them from working.

How they worked was told in a Stockholm report which appeared in the *Daily Telegraph* on October 2nd, 1939, entitled—"Sweden Meets Spy Menace," parts of which may be quoted by way of illustration.

"The Swedish police and military authorities, says the newspaper *Allehanda*, are organizing a special watch on Swedish ports following complaints of widespread espionage. Shipowners state that unless the menace is stamped out export trade will be quickly destroyed. Almost all Swedish shipping throughout the world is reported to be at a standstill.

" Military guards will probably be stationed at all ports, while detectives would watch foreign vessels and persons seeking to make contact with the crews. Business leaders and the general public have been warned to be careful to whom they communicate private information about the movements of Swedish ships.

"Shipowners say that not only in Swedish but also in Norwegian ports there are German spies who report the departure of every ship, and that German U-boat commanders have confirmed that they receive the fullest details of sailings in advance."

Following on this comes an account of the sinking of the S.S. *Nyland*, a Swedish vessel carrying five thousand three hundred tons of iron ore destined for steel works at Liege, Belgium. "The *Nyland* . . . was a neutral ship, which had left a neutral port for a neutral destination."

Against this may be set a quotation from a German propaganda article which appeared in the Madrid newspaper A.B.C. on September 16th, entitled "Gentlemanliness in War." It is remarked in the course of the article that "As the war gradually comes into perspective, the contrast between the conduct of the combatants becomes more obvious every day. This contrast may be pictured precisely in the weapons used by the belligerents. On the one side, Germany fights unprotected, launching her troops into the Polish battlefield. At sea her submarines pursue the enemy ships, never forgetting those annoying rules of war determined by International Law. . . . Before sinking a ship, the Germans give the crew time to escape and even help them to safety before firing the first torpedo. What is the response to this noble attitude? What weapons have been used up to now against Germany? Why is slander substituted for gunpowder? English aeroplanes have dropped millions and millions of leaflets on German soil, by which they try to separate Germans from their Fuehrer and from the National-Socialist régime freely adopted by the people. . . . Germany has never tried to separate the English people from their King, and here (in Berlin) it has caused great astonishment that anybody could believe it possible to separate Germans from their Leader."

If the sinking of a neutral ship, bound from one neutral country to another, constitutes "never forgetting those annoying rules of war determined by International Law," the difference between forgetfulness and practice requires no emphasis.

In Spain, Gestapo activities came to an end when the Civil War began: its beginning was the culmination of them. Thenceforth, in operations which were almost entirely political, the Nazi Party machine took over all operations in the country. That Gestapo penetration had been extensive may be judged from the fact that, in 1935 alone, the cost to Germany of maintaining its propaganda machinery in Spain was more than three and a half million pesetas.

With the victory of the Franco régime, controlled and supported as it was by German and Italian policy, material, and men, the chapter is closed. Work in the Peninsula is now, and for the future is intended to be, devoted to the underground control of Portugal. The long-standing friendship between that country and Britain is to be broken up, so that the whole of the peninsular west coast may be available for submarine bases at need. That is not to say that German vigilance in Spain is in any way relaxed. The Franco-controlled press of the country provides evidence to the contrary, any day. As in the last war, German exploits are extolled, British and French powers and resources are minimized—or ignored—and the possibility of Allied victory is never mentioned. For this type of work, the Gestapo is not needed; Nazi influence and propaganda are sufficient, combined as these are with the presence in the country of a multitude of German "technicians," and "advisers." The Liberal element, which might favour the Allied cause, is held down, and its voice stifled.

X

THE GESTAPO IN ENGLAND

ENGLAND, since the formation of the Gestapo, has been consistently regarded as the most difficult field of all in which to operate. A certain amount of work might be done, it was estimated, among the extremes of society, the lowest grades of the working-class population, and the semi-eccentrics and parasitic sections of the upper classes to whom new cults mean more than national interests —more than anything, in fact, since these people are eternally in quest of something which will either provide excitement or put their portraits in that section of the Press which chronicles their doings. But, between these two extremes, stands the great body of the middle classes, solidly imponderable, despised and hated by von Ribbentrop, and 99.9 per cent impervious to any influence the Gestapo could exert. Yet England has not escaped penetration.

Between 1934 and 1938, Gestapo agents of the type described in outlining German efforts in France were very busy in England. In particular, they carried out a number of economic and financial operations, working on a very large scale and making use of the international financial interests either centring or having establishments in London, and linking up the work done through these interests with that in Europe, to the detriment of English and especially of French finance. Complete records of these transactions are in the Gestapo archives in

Berlin, and they involve not only international, but British concerns, none of which had the slightest conception of the uses that were being made of them. As instance, the juggling which eventually crashed the Credit Anstalt in Vienna had definite and damaging repercussions on financial interests in this country: it was one among a number of transactions instigated and carried through by Gestapo agents of the finer sort.

In the discussions regarding England at the initial Gestapo conference in Munich, it was decided, for the reasons already given, that the methods to be pursued in Europe generally would not be applicable to England. In addition to this, the Nazi plans were so shaped—even by that time—that the country was considered as of less immediate importance than Central and Eastern Europe, and even of France and America. The place of England, in the Nazi scheme of things to be, was that of complete isolation, which was to be achieved by external means, not by work in England itself; thus the whole subject of Gestapo activities in the country was secondary to work on the Continent and in the States.

Still, certain agents, mostly minor ones—and, for the only time in Gestapo practice, women—were sent to England at different times and provided with the means of establishing small businesses, such as beauty parlours, manicure and hairdressing establishments, tobacco and newspaper shops, and the like, with the view of obtaining information that might give a lead in some definite direction. One of these came up for trial in the North when her activities were discovered—and when, in the view of the British Secret Service, she was of no further use in revealing her espionage contacts. Another, a supposedly Viennese fashion designer, achieved a greater measure of success, and, apparently, managed to keep her freedom. Of the vast measure of information secured by these and others, little was found to be of real value.

An apparently well-recommended and quite harmless youth—one of the Gestapo-trained ferrets —was enrolled in an English technical school with a view to his obtaining an appointment in the wireless service of the merchant marine, or at some important cable station, but he failed to get his appointment, and was recalled. Then the exchange of students between English and German universities was considered possible as a means of influencing certain phases of English life, but a detailed examination of this avenue of approach revealed it as disappointing. English university students, as a general rule, were hopelessly non-politically minded unlike their continental equivalents. From the German point of view, they were so stupidly insular that they resented any attempt at making them see English institutions and themselves as others— especially Germans—saw them. There were exceptions to this, like the Oxford leaders of the "won't fight whatever happens" movement, but most of these proved intractable, and resentful of any attempt, no matter how skilfully it might be made, to subvert them to Nazi uses. Their attitude was mainly a pose adopted for the sake of temporary notoriety: it had no foundation on which Gestapo work could be based, and the attempt at using them had to be abandoned.

Some small use was made of young German teachers of languages in England, both of those working in a private capacity and those attached to various schools of languages, and efforts in this direction were not altogether wasted. Far more use was made of Germans visiting the country, business and professional men, especially those whose mentality was less rigidly closed to foreign points of view than that of the average German. These were carefully sought out, and used. They had no specific mission beyond that of keeping their ears open, and the results obtained were well worth the trouble. There is probably—almost certainly, in fact—no people on earth so consistently and dangerously careless in their conversation as the English. Mothers will talk to any stranger about their sons in the Navy, Army, Air Force or merchant service, or in colonial posts. Where they are, what they are doing, where they are going—the minutest details will be discussed, and if "mother" has a bit of inside information of any sort, she pridefully displays her knowledge of the inner workings of things. Young men in bars and even in the street talk openly of where their brothers or friends are and what they are doing, wives tell of the whereabouts and work of their husbands, and fathers reveal that their sons are engaged either on work of national importance or in the services—all this with utter unrestraint, for all the world to hear.

If this appears an exaggeration, a case in point may be quoted. The war was well under way when a young officer of one of the Services, with enough of distinguishing badges on him for recognition, waited at a bus stop with an acquaintance or two, and talked while he waited, in such a way that everyone else could hear—fully a dozen people were there at the time. His remark—"Yes, we're off to Plymouth at six o'clock to-night," was audible to all the group—of which the present writer was one.

If any other there were a German agent, that remark was enough for deduction of the movement of a unit, and unostentatious following of the wide-mouthed one might reveal that unit's ultimate destination—and what else? Considerable reliance was placed by the Gestapo on a certain type of German refugee, as well as on Germans naturalized by marriage only, with a view to getting information that might be of value. The German mentality knows its own kind, and is convinced with some grounds that once a German always a German: sooner or later, it is believed, the most conscientious of exiles will work in the interests of the Fatherland. This belief was not unjustified; a constant trickle of information came, sometimes voluntarily, and sometimes with a little persuasion, from these people: often it gave a lead to things of importance.

For a long time, however, there was no attempt at establishing any network of espionage such as covered France. The economic and financial operations carried through by Gestapo manipulations in London were designed to further European political aims, rather than to cause harm to England itself, in which latter respect any effects the Gestapo agents might produce were incidental. There is reason to believe that the operations furthered the safe establishment in England of such Gestapo workers as controlled the organization in France, but to what extent the work of these men may be effective remains to be seen.

On the financial side, very efficient investigations were made as to the affairs of a number of German refugees in London who were suspected of removing property from the Reich, together with various international lawyers of German origin who were handling their business. It would probably surprise many of these people if they knew of the complete and detailed records of their transactions and private activities, in the hands of the Gestapo in Berlin.

Both Nazi and Gestapo policy in England were influenced by von Ribbentrop, who assured the Party time after time that he himself could deal fully and efficiently with its interests. This was the real purpose of his sojourn in England as Ambassador, while at the same time virtually acting as Foreign Minister—as witness his visits to Berlin to sign the German Pact with Japan, and his appointment to the Secret Council of Four while still accredited to London. He insisted on no interference of any kind with his plans, which were based on his determination to come to no terms with England, and to take any means that presented themselves of securing the ultimate humiliation of the country. With him, anglophobia is an obsession.

Steps were eventually taken for the establishment in England of such a system of espionage as covered France, though less money was spent than in that country, and the system therefore never attained such completeness. It was, however, established as planned, and particular attention was paid, as in France and Poland, to internal communications, the system of electrical distribution with locations of all its vital points, the congested railway junctions that feed London and the southern and eastern ports, the railways themselves, with special attention to the less-used lines of the Midlands, which in German estimation are strategic and in the event of war would carry the most important traffic from the North to London and the Channel ports. These last were very thoroughly mapped, together with junctions and sidings where concentrations might be expected, either of materials or of troops in movement.

Attention was also paid to the newly developing industrial areas of the Midlands, with a view to the location of targets for aerial attack. For some reason known to the Gestapo—probably to our own Secret Service as well, since its organization is far more thorough than is generally realized— Stratford-on-Avon and all the district between it and Bristol came in for a large share of the work done. The methods employed in French industrial espionage were followed, and the work was helped by the fact that large industrial concerns are often not centralized, but have auxiliary or shadow factories attached to them, with highly skilled men constantly moving from one establishment to another. Among those men, as is known now, were Gestapo agents, not infrequently of English birth.

If this last appears incredible, one has only to look back to the great strikes of 1921 and 1926, the first of which called for troop mobilization to prevent *English* agitators from wrecking the country, while the second was headed by well-known figures in public life who openly declared their intention of sabotaging government and assuming control of the country in the interests of only a section of its people. Since such men as Ramsay MacDonald and Snowden were capable of this, there is nothing incredible in the conversion of youngsters of the class from which these leaders of disruption arose— yet not so much conversion as a shaping of their discontents to Gestapo ends. That a number of them were so shaped and trained is incontestable, and they were planted in all vital industries, often in well-paid and important posts. The training was done as in France, and the trainees were—until they gave themselves away, as some have done—entirely above suspicion, appearing as cheery, contented souls, doing their work with the rest, and doing it well at that.

Unfortunately for their German employers, not all of their information can be turned to practical use: for instance, the exact formula for a new alloy of metals, designed to stand certain stresses under certain conditions, is not very useful if one of the components has to be *ersatz*, nor are the plans of a certain type of aeroplane of any great value as long as the materials available for construction will not admit of placing necessary strains on the completed machine. Because of things like these, Nazi propaganda is almost hysterical over the British blockade.

Little can be said as to Gestapo intervention in Ireland, though a good deal has been done there, and the course of events over a long period clearly indicates the aims to which the work has been directed. Chief among them has been that of fostering disagreement with England in every possible way—a task which has presented no great difficulties. In addition, steps have been taken to establish centres for espionage, the value of which in war is regarded as considerable. The work of the I.R.A. in England, consisting as it did of sabotage wherever it could be achieved, depended largely on German finance: it is to be noted that I.R.A. activities came to an abrupt end with the outbreak of war, German funds being no longer available to support them.

Irish elements in the U.S.A. have been carefully worked upon, ostensibly by compatriots in the home country, but in reality by the instigations of

Gestapo agents located there, with a view to influencing opinion against England, and that with no little success. Similar propaganda, only apparently of American–Irish origin, has been poured into Ireland from the States. The effectiveness of this may be gauged by a declaration of Mr. de Valera, to the effect that unless certain steps were taken against various leaders, civil strife would result. Whether mere civil strife or complete revolution suits the aims of the Gestapo is best known in Berlin: whatever the aim, neither pains nor money is stinted for its accomplishment.

As for Gestapo work in Great Britain itself, it has not been undetected, nor, after a month of war, were many of its agents left at large—though, as must be obvious, such as have not been rounded up are most dangerous. Here is the report of the initial round-up, issued during the first week of the war.

"Since the outbreak of hostilities the whole of Scotland Yard's detective department has been concentrated on the rounding-up of suspected enemy agents. More than 6,000 men and women are now detained in various parts of the country, a number of them British-born subjects.

"Scotland Yard, in conjunction with the Naval and Military intelligence departments, prepared the plans for the round-up some months ago, a list being compiled as follows:

Active enemy agents.
Persons suspected of acting as enemy agents.
Sympathizers likely to assist agents.

"The arrangements were so complete that, with few exceptions, every suspect whose name was on the list is now under detention.

"They will be detained throughout the war, and

it is unlikely that any of them will appear before a court. British subjects can appeal to the Home Secretary against detention, but must do so within ten days. The Home Secretary may then arrange for them to appear before a tribunal."

There is, in this, a reminiscence of the round-up with which war began in August 1914. At that time, though, there were no exceptions: the whole of the German spy system in England was destroyed, thanks to Ernst's "post office." The superiority of the Gestapo system to that of which Ernst was part is evidenced by the fact of "a few exceptions," for the time being. Not for long.

XI

THE U.S.A. CAMPAIGN

EARLY in 1934, four Gestapo agents were sent to New York, travelling from Genoa in an Italian ship. They were the most carefully chosen, the most completely and meticulously trained, and in every way the most efficient of all workers that were sent out by the Gestapo centre in the Sudetenland: considered as a unit, they made the most effectively ruthless, conscienceless, and anti-social propaganda machine that the best minds of the Gestapo could fashion.

They understood to the full the magnitude of the task to which they went, and were letter-perfect in the use of a technique which, although it was to be employed at so great a distance from the control to which they had been accustomed, would be operated by them with a finesse and skill which would make von Papen's former efforts in the United States appear crude and haphazard by comparison. The leader of the party was of Bulgarian nationality; he had acquired his education in Vienna, Milan, Paris, and Lyons, and had been trained by the Gestapo mentors in Teplitz-Schönau, while he had also undergone a course at the American College at Stamboul. He was not twenty-three when he set out from Genoa; his companions, of about the same age or even younger, were outwardly attractive and rather ingenuous youths, as was he; behind the façade of them all was a sophistication and know-

244

ledge of the world utterly at variance with their years.

They landed in America with Czech passports, taking with them introductions, the addresses of contacts they must make, and a specialized knowledge of the field of their operations not less complete than that provided for Gestapo workers in France, notwithstanding the fact that the controllers who had sent them out had no personal knowledge of the States. How this was achieved needs a fairly detailed explanation.

The first question to be considered was the vast amount of territory to be covered, and to decide whether this would involve the use of a large number of workers, since any plan calling for the use of numbers would present difficulties. A country comparable with Europe for size, in which it was possible to make through railway journeys of 4,000 miles, which meant that the distance between New York and some of the western cities was greater than that between New York and any point in Europe, implied the use of a vast horde of agents to obtain any results worth considering, unless there were other means of reaching essential contacts without continual travelling. Two alternative methods were clearly seen: national unions of Labour, and national organizations of the professional classes, the business communities, and also of American women, who are intensely active and enthusiastic, and who bring together all sections and classes of American life in State and National conventions and meetings, so frequently and comprehensively that the difficulty of reaching them is minimized, if not altogether obviated.

The second, complementary alternative was considered even more useful. In the United States there are a large number of very clearly defined and politically powerful racial organizations which, properly approached, would make fertile ground for propaganda of every kind. The purely German organizations were financially and economically influential, and that of the Czechs, with some 40,000 members, almost equally so. It was, finally, through organizations of this latter type that the plans for work in the States were completed, and the methods used savoured more of intrigue, bribery, and betrayal than even the normal Gestapo technique, which is saying a good deal.

It was known to the Gestapo controllers of activities outside Germany that the Czech Central Government in Prague conducted a considerable amount of propaganda work in America, and that this had been founded in the first place by the President and his Foreign Minister, both before and during the last war. A great deal of money had been spent on developing the organization which conducted this propaganda, and through American-Czech institutions, with the co-operation of American educational interests, it was directed not only through the usual political channels, but also through the medium of the schools. Two officials connected with the organization at the Czecho-Slovak end were selected by the Gestapo, and for various reasons, by means of bribes and knowledge of details of their private lives which could be used as blackmail, they were forced to betray the secrets of their work.

One of these was a high official in the department of finance in Prague, the other an equally highly placed individual in the department concerned with education. The latter was also a controlling figure of propaganda disseminated by means of the Czech

youth organizations known as "Sokols" (Falcons).
It was intended to spread Czech influence among
American youth circles, with a view to establishing
"Sokols" among Czech-American groups in the
States. These, in turn, would work for the Czech
Republic in Europe, and spread Czech influence
among American youth of other origins—convert
the German-born, perhaps.

The official of the finance department was
naturally in a position to pass on complete information as to the identities and positions of his correspondents in the States, and to explain the method
of procedure for his side of the dissemination of
propaganda. All the information supplied to the
Gestapo was sifted and studied, and it was noted
that much of the work was done by use of the
American system of municipal administration and
its powerful political ramifications. Through these
latter it was possible to influence not only social,
commercial, and judicial interests, but also the trend
of state politics, and through a combination of the
four possible to exert influence and even pressure
on various departments of the Federal authority.

Evidence was obtained to show that the Czech
propaganda machine had made a good deal of use of
these means, and had interests and connections
throughout America. Complete details were given
to the Gestapo of the liaison existing between
Prague and many important American cities. As an
example, a very detailed investigation was made into
the results obtained between 1931 and 1933, when a
Czech-American was mayor of Chicago. In In-
dianapolis and Pittsburg, to mention two other
centres, Czech interests had undoubtedly been able
to exert influence on the municipal authorities, and
from the mass of information of which these details

were part, the ground was prepared for the Gestapo
campaign in the U.S.A.

Everything that could be of value to the men sent
over was summarized and tabulated for their use;
they were furnished with full details of the internal
organization and working of the American bunds;
lists of men and women who could be used were
made for them. Commercial and financial interests
on which pressure could be brought to bear by
means of the knowledge thus acquired, and politicians who had dabbled in propaganda to an extent
that rendered them likely of access, were listed.
Personal introductions to prominent and influential people were obtained, no matter in what sphere
of American life the interests of these people lay;
they included men and women in a score of the
principal American cities, and the introductions
ensured that the Gestapo men would be received in
circles worth their attention, at every strategic point
between New York and the Pacific coast.

Introductions were also obtained to ensure reception of the four by American citizens of German,
Czech, and other European origins. These were
furnished by relatives in the home countries of the
people concerned, by university professors to their
opposite numbers in American educational establishments, business men with interests in the States,
and others. Every possible preparation was made to
secure advantages which the Gestapo agents might
use, and in that respect they set out quite as fully
prepared as those whose work lay in countries
adjacent to or near the Reich.

The method of working was to be similar to that
which characterized Gestapo work in France, with
such modifications as suited the conditions known
to exist in the States. The value of the material put

at the disposal of these agents is self-evident, and, trained as they were to use it, no more dangerously effective group of personnel could have been let loose on an unsuspecting community than that of the four suave and easy-mannered young men who arrived in New York early in 1934.

It was not to be and was not expected that any spectacular results would be immediately forthcoming from the venture; the four had a vast amount of preliminary survey work to do, but they were completely trusted by the Gestapo control, and were hampered by no limitations of supervision, nor of finance. The whole knowledge and unstinting help of the German diplomatic and consular services in the States was at their command at all times, and nothing they could ask would be refused, since with every Nazi German, at home or abroad, the Gestapo is resistless.

From the day of their arrival at New York, these four exponents of Himmler's foul ruthlessness were absorbed into the life and activities of the American people, and became an integral and ever increasing power in American institutions—a power rendered more formidable by the fact that it was secret, even unsuspected as being one. The success which rewarded their efforts may be judged from the fact that it was never found necessary to send other agents of the same type to America.

The operations they had to achieve were not so varied in nature as those of similar agents in Western Europe—France, for instance. Any actual military invasion of the United States has, naturally, never been even remotely considered as possible by Germany, and thus military espionage on the von Fritsch plan was not considered necessary, even less so when exchange of knowledge and aims between

the German and Japanese General Staffs revealed
the thoroughness with which this branch of
espionage had been supplied by the latter. Espionage in and of the American Navy and mercantile
marine, however, was extensively undertaken, and
that part of the general system which involved the
recruiting of sub-agents in the country received very
careful attention, with a view to the creation of an
effective force of workers in all departments of the
nation's industries and commercial undertakings.

This last was intended to ensure full information
of and systematic and effective sabotage in industries
and in the merchant shipping in the possible event
of the entry of the United States to a European war,
although the Nazi triumvirate regarded such a possibility as very remote. United States fears of intensive bombardment from the air, by planes from
groups of aeroplane carriers off the coast, were quite
unfounded, though in the distant future such a
possibility might become reality if the successive
stages of Nazi policy could be realized until only the
American continent remained to be subjugated. By
that time, if all the plans worked out in accordance
with the hopes behind them, all South America
would be Nazified and friendly, and the United
States would come into the Nazi fold without being
bombed. Is there any need to insist yet again that
the German mentality is incapable of comprehending the reactions of other nations to any given event
or activity?

Another important part of the work of the four
agents was that of helping in every way, principally
by liaison and intrigue, the growth of German-
American political organizations, and to direct by
every possible means Irish-American sympathy to
support of the German section of the nation. In the

latter field, considerable success has attended their efforts.

The importance attached to this side of the work may be gauged by the dispatch of Captain Weidemann, one of Hitler's personal advisers and "reporters," to America with the somewhat obscure position of Consul-general at San Francisco. This appointment was altogether misunderstood both in France and England; it was regarded as disposing of Weidemann, a sort of reduction from his high estate, when in reality it was a position of great responsibility.

Political bickerings between the Reich and the United States, which resulted in the nominal recall of their respective ambassadors, was not regarded in Berlin as a serious setback. Nazi aims require the neutrality of the United States, and its policy is to ensure that neutrality. To that end, it relies to a great extent on the "menace" of Japan. The exigencies of the situation in the Far East are calculated by Berlin to direct the attention of the States to the Pacific coast, and any withdrawal of English or French naval forces, consequent on abandonment of their Chinese interests, or by reason of war in Europe, would, it is anticipated, only increase the anxiety and responsibilities of America in the Pacific. Japan's defiance of American wishes and even veiled threats of war were designed solely to further this purpose. Japanese plans for expansion may not be limited to the Far East; in the German plan of things to be, Japan's objective is Australia, which is intended to provide living space for the superabundant population for which room cannot be found in crowded China, even if complete conquest of that country could be achieved. Without that fresh living space, German propagandists drip into the willing ears of the Japanese, their very existence as a nation is threatened. And the intensive and known Japanese espionage in America is a measure, not of Japan's aggressive intentions, but of her fear of American intervention to prevent the accomplishment of her Far Eastern and Australian aims.

This digression may help to make clear how it was that the Gestapo agents took little interest in actual military espionage. That they have taken steps to ensure efficient work in that direction in the event of war may be taken for granted, but it would in all probability not be set in action until the new armies of the United States were in process of formation, when the system of naval, merchant marine, and "communications" espionage already formed would act in conjunction with the military side, and not, as now, independently.

Sabotage in all branches of industry connected with the production of war material is already organized, against the possibility of the United States taking part in a European war, when the plans would be translated into action. This would not be the crude explosions and wanton, even futile destruction of von Papen's organizing, but sabotage scientifically planned and skilfully carried out, until the highly qualified workmen and technicians responsible for it could be traced down—which they and their Gestapo organizers believe to be impossible. It would consist in unexplainable defects in highly important metal alloys; in the engines and fabric of aeroplanes, the breech mechanism of guns, the fallibility of altimeters and range-finders of all kinds, the propeller shafts of ships. Ammunition of all sorts would prove ineffective, consignments of essential component parts would be deflected and lost, stores and foodstuffs misdirected and jettisoned as spoiled. Wireless communications would break down inexplicably, and both internal and external communications would be subject to delay. With this sort of sabotage in full blast, Gestapo agents would begin work on the political fabric of the country through internal dissatisfaction, distrust, suspicion of graft, and the inevitably following agitation. It is in preparation for this last that the whole of the work has been planned and organized, against the possible need.

Fantastic! Impossible! Yet Germans, many of them German-born, constitute ten per cent of the total population of America, and ever the German turns back to the Fatherland, puts it before all, works for it, and with "Deutschland uber alles" drummed into him and his fathers for the past seventy years, with the vision of world-conquest put before his eyes once again—is it so fantastic? Is it so impossible? While Prussianism survives to pervert the German nation to evil, no evil is impossible, no scheme for the accomplishment of evil fantastic.

The four original agents of 1934, five years older now, and just that much more experienced and therefore dangerously efficient, are still at work, and the exact extent of the hidden ramifications of Gestapo activities in America are known to one man only—Himmler, the inscrutable, passionless, conscienceless Chief of the Secret Police. His cynical half-smile and cold eyes betray nothing as he sits at his enormous desk in Wilhelmstrasse 77, Berlin, W.8.

XII

LIAISON WITH FASCISM

THROUGH liaison with the Italian Secret
Police, Gestapo operations were begun on
North Africa by way of Italy. From Libya they
branched east and west, the eastern activities reaching to Egypt, Tanganyika (formerly German East
Africa, and still with a percentage of Germans
among its white population), the Cape, India and
Ceylon, and on to Sourabaya in Java, where they
linked up with Japanese penetration; westward they
went out to Casablanca, Dakar in French Senegal,
and across the South Atlantic to South America.

The Gestapo did not at first work independently,
but in conjunction with the Italian Secret Police,
which had already penetrated into many of the
territories that would be in the anticipated and
logical line of advance of the reconstituted German
Intelligence Service. Collaboration between Italy
and the Reich was in no way due to Hitler's accession to power: he had been in the closest touch
with Mussolini and the Fascist propaganda elements
since 1929. The policy of the National Socialist
Party was not shaped solely on *Mein Kampf* and
Hitler's dreams—not even when these were reinforced by Hitler's emotional storms and Hitler's
tears. It was backed by the solid experience of the
Duce and his castor oil campaign against opposition.
Hitler's idealist views on world domination through
the regeneration of youth fitted in very nicely with

the Fascist idea of domination by any means at all, even if they did not go so far—as castor oil, for instance.

The party had, then, not only received constant help from its opposite number in Italy, but had pledged itself to future co-operation in the pursuit of certain aims common to both, aims which Italy was not strong enough to bring to fruition alone. Hitler was not the only one with a fanatical determination to wipe out the Versailles "Diktat": the Duce had not forgotten that the representative of Italy had walked out from the Hall of Mirrors and turned his back on Versailles, in bitter protest over the unsavoury scraps that were flung to his country out of the scramble which characterized that feast. A "Fascist" Germany rising from the ashes of defeat, a Germany which had forbidden the use of the word "verlag" (treaty) in connection with Versailles, and substituted "diktat" would be a useful aide—and dictators do not give their help for nothing. At that time, Mussolini probably did not see that Germany would rise with such phoenix-like strength and become his master.

Also, in outlining his plans for world domination in concert with Italy, Hitler probably forgot to mention that he regarded Italy as part of the Holy Roman Empire, which had often, if not always, had a German Emperor.

The internal organizations of the National Socialist Party had received a useful quantity of lists and other help from the Italian Secret Police, and prior to 1932, when the Gestapo was formed, Goebbels had set Heinrich Himmler to study the Fascist police constitution and methods—a provision which Roehm had neglected to make for himself. When the time came for the Gestapo to reach across the Mediterranean to Africa, the logical, obvious way was through Italy. Thus the Italian Secret Police were useful, up to a point—and the Gestapo never bothered itself about anybody or anything except with a view to use. And, just as Mussolini was to become an adjunct of the Fuehrer, so the Italian Police were to be virtually a department of the Gestapo; by 1934 their internal activities in Italy had been reshaped by Himmler.

The conquest of Abyssinia was undertaken as the first step in the joint world-domination plan, since it affected the Far East. A base on the other, far side of Egypt, was essential, and Italian Somaliland was inadequate. The barren empire of the Lion of Judah was not worth German blood—hardly worth Italian, for that matter—for itself alone: this, of course, from Goering's point of view. The time was not far distant when Herman Goering was to ride through the streets of Rome, his white uniform slashed and blazoned with the crimson and blue and gold of the Papal Orders of the Holy Roman Empire, his baton ablaze with the jewels of Imperial Austria—and his mind already occupied with the idea of kings and Pope as pawns to be moved at will—his will!

Thus the Gestapo examined the work of the Italian Secret Police, took it to pieces, and put it together again in a shape that would serve Nazi ends as well as those of the Duce. Gestapo technique was far finer, far more efficient, and for this reason Gestapo control was not resented—this in the same way that Mussolini realized the German General Staff as necessary for the shaping of his armies.

So far as secret police work, as Germany and Himmler conceived it, on the southern side of the Mediterranean was concerned, a considerable amount had already been done by Italians, and some results had been obtained through the Italians settled in Tunisia and French Morocco, especially in the former territory. In the political field, the scant Italian knowledge of native mentalities, and of Arab and Egyptian projects and aims, had permitted of very slight progress only. A more specialized knowledge and a more efficient technique was necessary, and this the Gestapo would supply. The field of operations was vast, the opportunities almost limitless. From Egypt, first to be attacked, they would spread down the east coast of Africa to link up with the operations based in German South-west Africa (as the Reich still regarded it) beyond the Cape, whence the Union of South Africa might be seduced from even the shadow of alliance with England. The turbulent and easily-stirred Arab populations on the eastern shores of the Red Sea and to the south of it would be controlled from a different direction (that is, Gestapo work on them would) but the main line of advance would stretch on to India, beginning first in the industrial cities of Bombay and Calcutta, while at the same time Afghanistan and the former Baluchistan must be wooed. Thence to Java, where the Japanese Secret Service would link up. In the opposite direction from its Libyan base, to the west, Gestapo agencies would be reinforced by Spanish aid at Casablanca, go on to Dakar, and thence stretch out to take in the South American republics.

This followed the general aims of the Nazi Party; the place that Italy would fill in the general scheme of things had been decided. Always there was the probability—in Hitler's own mind not merely a hope, but nearly a certainty, that no major war

would be necessary. He believed that France and
England would defer action until it was too late;
Goering and the Prussian leaders were not so sure,
but they trusted to their own ability—backed by a
few of Adolf's tears, perhaps—to hoodwink the
democratic powers and accomplish their own plans
to such an extent that, when England and France
realized the necessity for resistance against German
might, they would also realize that making war
would only hasten the inevitable end. It was one
more instance of German inability to estimate the
tempers of other nations, or to see in advance the
reactions of non-German peoples to German megalomania.

If, however, war could not be avoided, Prussianism planned to localize it, and by the intensive
measures designed by General von Fritsch to make
it of short duration. The technique of the "blitz-
krieg" demanded war on only one front at a time,
and the whole of the alleged and flaunted naval and
military might of Italy was designed for one purpose
only, that of frightening the rest of Europe into
neutrality while Germany crushed England and
France. Meanwhile, to the south of the Mediterranean, the Gestapo had the advantage of all preliminary work done by the Italian Secret Police, to
which they added their own technique.

The most superficial student of the situation may
recall how, ever since the Nazi Party came to power
in Germany, France has had to face and deal with
Italian claims in Tunisia, attempts at giving the
"planted" Italian communities a share in the control of the country, and Italian threats which compelled the establishment of a strong line of defence
along the Libyan frontier. Trace back these persistent demands and threats to their source, and

that source is not Mussolini or Fascism, but Himmler at his desk in Berlin. It is an adaptation of the Gestapo tactics pursued in Czecho-Slovakia. The personal knowledge of these countries and of the East possessed by the Gestapo control of operations outside Germany was the directive element in these operations, though the amount of work to be done was not large. This will be clear if the general Nazi plan is considered as a whole: in Africa itself, it was designed to penetrate and eventually dominate the Union of South Africa, the strongest anti-Nazi part of the continent, and to "encircle" Egypt. The former, it was estimated, could be accomplished in time by means of propaganda from Tanganyika through the German racial element which had never been ousted from that colony, and the Union itself was, in the German view, as vulnerable from a military point of view as Czecho-Slovakia had proved: Boer and Afrikander could be subverted from any English leanings, and such a rebellion as that which occurred during the last war—but far better organized and more efficiently financed—could be brought about.

Egypt, threatened from Libya on the west, and with its communications to southward cut from Abyssinia, would form no serious obstacle, it was anticipated. None of this was to be undertaken until the general plan had been advanced to a point at which swollen Germany was ready to swallow Africa. Prussianism must first be dominant in Europe, and Japan must advance as far westward as Java in order to cover the operations through which it would obtain Australia, coveted "lebensraum." At that point, in the German view of things, all Africa would be theirs for the taking. In the meantime, the ground both there and in India could be prepared by adaptation of the normal Gestapo methods.

The usual procedure of propaganda by Nazi Party agents and Gestapo penetration into commerce and industry was followed. Nazi Party work was mainly centred in South-west Africa, the former German colony, with a view to the eventual seduction of the Union: taken on the whole, it did not work very well, and the Union's declaration of solidarity with Great Britain and the rest of the Dominions came as a grievous disappointment to Goering and the rest of the Nazi chiefs. Gestapo work was spread throughout Egypt and the French colonies, while in India and Burma existing German and Italian commercial concerns were used—the extensive Italian colony and shipping interests in Alexandria proved very useful—while the factories and selling organization of a very large, foreign-owned manufacturing concern also served as bases.

Among the politically turbulent factions of India the work of spreading disaffection and the seeds of revolt was not considered difficult. At Casablanca in Spanish Morocco, the Gestapo had established headquarters for its operations in Spain as early as 1934, and the post was maintained until the course of events in Spain rendered it superfluous. Attention was then turned to Dakar, in French Senegal, from which point contact was maintained with the South American organizations: thence, too, propaganda was controlled in Portugal, in the Canaries, and Madeira.

Later, all this work was again to be centred in and directed from Spain itself. With the success of General Franco, Germany could regard' every department of the Spanish national administration as thoroughly penetrated: if the Gestapo had no

actual control of things, it had at least a rather
authoritative voice in every key office of the new
Government. Spanish influence in South America
has always been considerable, and now, directed by
the Gestapo, it could be used with intensity to
further German aims. The need for secrecy is
practically non-existent, and the campaign is almost
as open as it is intense. The effectiveness of the
methods employed, and proof of the Gestapo's
power to influence public opinion both in Spain and
South America, is evident both in the Spanish and
South American press, and in radio broadcasts.
In South America, both Nazi Party and Gestapo
activities were very quickly successful. Conditions,
especially in Brazil and Argentina, were eminently
suited to the progress of the work: it is not
generally realized in Europe how very thoroughly
Nazi influences have penetrated these countries.
The damage done is probably appreciated by the
United States Government, members of which had
every opportunity of appreciating it at the last
Pan-American Congress held at Quito, which city
decorated itself for the occasion with swastika flags.
It may be remembered that the implication of a
threat to the United States from the south was one
of the objectives of Nazi policy: this, combined with
the Japanese shadow in the west, was to absorb the
U.S.A. in its own affairs and the protection of its
own borders, so that England might be completely
isolated and expect no aid from the west.

In the majority of South American countries, and
particularly in Brazil and Argentina, large German
colonies exist. They have never been fully absorbed
into the life and economy of the countries concerned, as have Italian immigrants, but have remained definite and separate entities. Not only this,

but through their financial and political unity they have secured for themselves a considerable amount of control over their own affairs; they have maintained their own schools, staffed by German teachers, and with the German language as the medium for instruction. These German colonies were subjected as soon as possible to Nazi propaganda, which was maintained ceaselessly, and organizers were sent from the Sudetenland to form the usual party organizations of youths of both sexes, and of the women. The usual Gestapo operations for penetration of the internal economy of each country were set in movement, and the usual intrigue in political and commercial circles was undertaken with a view to influencing affairs always in the direction favourable to National Socialism, and against democracy and its tenets as represented by the United States.

The Gestapo could extend its operations no farther to the west: when Quito took to swastikas, the Pacific Ocean had been reached. On the other side of the world, it had also reached its limit when the post established as headquarters at Sourabaya made contact with the Japanese—as had been arranged with Japanese emissaries in Teplitz-Schönau not long after the beginning of things, when the policy of linking up with the two potentially great military powers who wanted—or thought they wanted—"lebensraum" was adopted by the Reich. All three suffered from this complaint, or hypochondriacally believed they did, and thus they became bedfellows. Whether two of them have finally decided to get out of bed and look round for themselves remains, at this present time, to be seen: signs of something of the sort are not wanting.

The aims and operations of the Gestapo, now dotted over all the countries of the Near and Middle East, and practically encircling Africa, have been "surveyed," necessarily in very brief outline— this is intended as a single book, not as a library. The work has gone on year by year since 1932, with the patient and meticulous thoroughness and attention to detail which is characteristically German— and, in this case, very Prussian indeed. From the Prussian point of view, the ground is all prepared, but the final stages of the work must wait on events in Europe. If, at this present stage (early October 1939) France and England can be persuaded to cut their own throats by concluding peace with a Nazi Germany, then beyond question Prussianism will eventually come to complete dominance in Europe. Then the word will go out, and swift and startling changes will take place almost simultaneously throughout Africa and the East. Political domination and economic dictation will be imposed on South America, and, lastly, attention will be turned to the United States and Canada.

Improbable—yes. But not yet beyond possibility, little as the average democratic citizen would care to admit anything of the sort. It is not merely improbable, but impossible, that, in a world which has attained to modern standards of civilization, it should be necessary to put over six millions of men under arms, and maintain them in the field at the cost of millions sterling per day, merely to assert the principles by which freedom of thought, word, and action are maintained. Quite impossible—but true! Against them and their effort, in Hitler's own words—"The National Socialist Movement is therefore not the preserver of the countries of the past, but their liquidator in favour of the Reich of the future." All—ALL!—are to be liquidated and made tributary to the Reich.

Hitler's dream: for seventy years and more, Prussia's aim.

One final word with regard to Gestapo propaganda in the southern half of the American continent. If Hildegarde Heinrich, sister of Marie Heinrich of Teplitz-Schönau, can be found in any one of the South American republics, then she should be stamped on and obliterated, regardless of sex or human sympathies, as the initial disseminatress of the Nazi poison that has been instilled into the women of every South American state. Gestapo-trained, she is dangerous as is a venomous snake, and as such should be attacked.

XIII

CHEZ HIMMLER

IN the foregoing pages, the external activities of
the GEheim STAats POlizei of the Third Reich
have been surveyed in outline. Probably a good
many popular conceptions of what the Gestapo is
and what it does have been blown sky high, but
that is inevitable. It must by now be clear that the
Gestapo does not consist of a horde of spies of the
type beloved by the late William le Queux, but of a
few very highly trained and ruthlessly efficient
agents, carefully chosen, each one of whom is
capable of penetrating every phase of a nation's life
and economy. And such a body of men as that is a
far more dangerous thing.

The Gestapo as organized for work in the Reich
itself comes much nearer to the popular conception
of what it ought to be. It certainly has a horde of
spies, and in every walk of life at that. They are
rendered necessary by the fact that the Gestapo has
two functions to fulfil—or rather, that its operations call for two different kinds of activity. The
first is the constant surveillance of all administrative
departments and their officials, of high personages,
of financial and industrial operations, and of curb-
ing ambitions of leaders in every department and
preserving a balance of power. This requires
intrigue conducted by the usual Gestapo method
and technique. The second is that of keeping constant watch on the people generally, and not only

checking all subversive movements and elements, but observing the results of Nazi Party propaganda and detecting errors of method. This calls for no intrigue, and is done purely and simply by an army of spies.

Even so, the Gestapo does not maintain an enormous staff for either purpose. The first is done by highly trained, efficient agents, and the second by the people themselves, without any great expense. The fear of the Gestapo and its omniscience is so deeply instilled into the German mind that in all classes of the people men, women, and children spy on one another for their own safety.

The Gestapo has its finger not only on the pulse of the German nation as a whole, but on every individual and in every home from the Rhine to the Polish border, from the Baltic shore to the southern frontier. There is literally nothing that escapes its notice, and nothing that it does not use to its own ends.

There is no department of the national life which it does not watch closely and supervise, and its power is unlimited. It does not run the concentration camps; that is done by the Nazi Party, which supplies the "force" when it is needed: the Gestapo may help to fill the camps. It does, however, run the prisons, or certain of them, and they are much more secret than the camps.

Himmler, the head of the Gestapo, is responsible to nobody except Hitler: that is, in theory. Actually, the direction of things is in the hands of Goering, but the Gestapo has to render no account of itself or its work to any department of the State or to the Government as a whole. It acts solely on its own authority, and its decisions and actions need no confirmation or countersigning by any authority at all, political, administrative, or legal. It can move in any field and intervene in any way with a finality from which there is no appeal: this with the power vested in its own authority alone.

Standing quite apart from all this is the department which controls operations outside Germany. This, as has already been noted, is divided into three sections: the Western Division at Cologne, the Eastern Division at Dresden, and the Military and Naval Division at Magdeburg. The three sections came into existence in 1935, and, as the organization of the Gestapo's external work proceeded and each piece was fitted to its place, it was handed over to the appropriate control.

They are intriguingly interesting places, these models of German organization, thoroughness, and efficiency. All three are constituted on the same lines and work in the same way. The Eastern Division occupies a building in the Pragerstrasse at Dresden; the military and naval headquarters is located in an annexe of the administrative building belonging to the civil industries department of the Krupp works at Magdeburg, and the Western Division has its headquarters at 26, Salier Ring, Cologne. To describe one is to picture all three, so far as organization and system are concerned.

Each has, however, a differing clientele. The Gestapo foreign agents very rarely appear at any one of the three places; they seldom leave the countries to which they have been posted, and Germany is not the direction in which they go, as a rule. Few native Germans have business in these silent, secretive-looking buildings. If a German citizen is summoned to any one of the three, he can regard the summons as, long ago, people regarded a *lettre de cachet*. It probably means that the Gestapo has learned through its foreign services, or in other ways, of some activities with which that particular German in the Reich is connected, or on which he can throw some light. If that is so, he is not summoned by letter, but a forceful-looking youth appears at his home, his office—even his bedside in some instances—and his friends lose sight of him. Unless they too are implicated and swept into the net, they never learn where he went, or why.

Visitors common to all three of these establishments—that is, in type only—are foreigners, men and women of obviously every class from aristocrat to labourer, but all of them rather furtive and nervous. At Dresden they are from Eastern Europe and the Balkans, the Middle East, and Egyptians and Orientals may be seen at times. At Cologne they are Spanish, French, English, and other Western types. They are all citizens of some foreign country or other, and each one of them has something for sale: the transactions which take place behind the closed doors of the buildings in the Pragerstrasse, the Krupp Avenue, or the Salier Ring brand them as traitors, to be trusted not even by their new masters.

They all find the way to the particular headquarters concerned with the information by the same means, though not by the same route. A person who discovers something which might be of value to a foreign power has only to seek out its embassy or one of its consulates. If an embassy, he is put on to the first military attaché or the first secretary, according to the nature of the information he has to sell: only these two officials have authority to deal with him. If he goes to a consulate only the consul can act. Sufficient questions are put to the man to get an idea of the relative importance of his information and to which department, economic or military, it might be of use. If he tries to be fully informative, he is discouraged from it, and asked if he is willing to go to Germany, taking with him whatever it is he has to sell, and if he is not willing, every kind of persuasion is used to make him so, beginning with the direct statement that, in case he will not go, nothing can be done. The last thing that the official concerned is instructed to do is to let the man go without coming to a definite decision, but under no circumstances would the embassy or consulate negotiate the deal, or put the vendor in touch with an agent in the country concerned.

Another feature of these proceedings is that the man will be trapped, somehow, into admitting that he is acting from sympathy with National Socialist ideals, or from purposes of revenge—anything except for money, although it is stressed that he will receive his expenses on a liberal scale, including—if he needs them—railway and steamer tickets to Germany. Even a passport will be found for him if the matter appears of enough importance, and he is told to arrive at a certain town—never Berlin or Cologne—and go to a certain address at a given time. There he is met and questioned, and taken, say, to Cologne. This procedure is adopted because unknown to the man himself, his finger-prints and a dozen photographs of him will be taken, and a minute description recorded for the Gestapo dossiers. He will be completely compromised, so that proof of his acts that day could be produced at any time, and thus, if he were ever needed again, he would have to go.

Assuming that he had no passport, and the matter were not important enough to call for the issue of one, he would, if he belonged to a Western country, be sent with a week-end ticket to France or Belgium, and instructed at which inconspicuous hotel to stay, at which he would be met. His type— very seldom "her" type—can often be seen at any of the three discreet-looking buildings in Germany. No attempt to protect any one of these traitors by secrecy or in any other way is made: the idea is to compromise them in every possible way. From the moment any one of them reaches the frontier of the Reich, he is kept under close observation, and it may be said that the number of them is far from few. They go to Cologne from west and south and north, to Magdeburg from every direction, to Dresden from the east. There are exceptions: Amsterdam has always been the venue for meetings between the Western divisional chiefs and important visitors who do not wish to enter Germany; Prague or Teplitz-Schönau were used in the same way by Dresden. This last-named city may be approached by rail from the south, east, or west, coming from Bohemia; by way of the River Elbe, by the inter-sected road which crosses the frontier at Boden-bach, or by the narrow mountain road that winds through the pass of Zinnwald, some 5,000 feet above sea level.

This Zinnwald road was the *via dolorosa* of the Czech Republic. Along it, in both directions, moved the Gestapo-instigated forces that destroyed the State. It leads due south from Dresden, and goes up through the foothills of the Erzegebirge range to Zinnwald, some seventeen to twenty miles. Then it descends in a great, winding curve through the dense pine and oak forests of the southern slopes to Teplitz-Schönau, fourteen miles from the summit of the pass. Dotted about these same slopes are still the huts and cabins and old houses used by Kuehnel's Sudeten youths as hostels; through them were smuggled the weapons and ammunition with which all the Sudeten youth were armed. At Teplitz-Schönau the road becomes the Mazarykstrasse, and passes the Café Kreutz and Marie Heinrich's apartment, where the Committee of Five for the destruction of the Czech State used to meet. It leads past the School of Ceramics, to continue through the very centre of the fortified zone of Teresienstadt and the triple ring of the Prague defences, entering the city by way of a quiet and respectable suburb.

The Gestapo at one time instituted a service of passenger omnibuses along this road, which connected at Zinnwald with a similar service from Dresden. The vehicles rarely seemed to have any accommodation for merely idle or uninterested passengers. The Czech official of the Ministry of Transport, who—very discreetly—put through the transport concession for this purpose, refrained from inquiring closely into the reasons for the apparently not very necessary bus service.

A similar road, in some respects, leads to Cologne, but the principal line of approach there is by the network of railways which give access to the city from every direction. The Gestapo guides who conducted the foolish dupes with their hopes of reward always paused in the big square, just outside the railway station, and pointed out the magnificent frontage of the cathedral, with its intricate tracery appearing as delicate as the finest fretwork, but giving, nevertheless, an impression of soaring, mighty solidity. They seemed always to think that, with this, their duties to the visitors as far as Cologne, the city, was concerned had been carried out—and now for business.

The tramways of Cologne extend in all directions with—for a stranger—bewildering junctions at street corners. The city itself is spaciously and well laid out with broad, tree-lined streets, all very straight and formal-looking: its periphery is encircled by great avenues, somewhat in the manner of Paris—over six millions sterling of English and American money went to the development of these and other constructions of this one city, in the days after the last war when Germany pleaded utter starvation as a reason for evasion of its debts.

Salier Ring is one of these encircling avenues, and number twenty-six is a big, grey building with great double doors in its frontage: down one side of the doorway is a series of bell-pushes. If the wrong one is pressed, nothing happens—but this does not often occur, because all strangers to the place are personally conducted there. If the right bell is rung a little whirring sound precedes the automatic opening of one of the doors, which reveals a quite bare entrance hall, containing a staircase, but apparently no doors.

Nobody will appear in this hall: a curiously heavy silence characterizes it, so that footsteps on the bare stone flooring seem deadened: the Gestapo knows the value of initial impressions. A visitor's guide takes him straight to the only room in the building that he will see; if he had a chance of inspecting others, he would find them all exactly alike both as regards furnishing and occupancy, unless he descended from any one of the four upper floors to the basement of the building.

At each floor the staircase gives on to a bare corridor from which doors open on each side and at equal intervals: at each end of the corridor is a tall window, not made to open, but barred both outside and in. Both the corridor and the doors give an impression of silent blankness, and the particular door to which the visitor is conducted will depend entirely on the department concerned with his information. In any case, either at Cologne or Dresden, it will be of an economic kind, affecting finance, shipping, factories or industrial secrets—anything except actual military or naval information, all of which goes to Magdeburg—and in each of these three places the organization is exactly similar.

The visitor to Cologne or Dresden may have plans in his pocket, not of forts or gun emplacements, but of the layout and site of some factory or engineering works, or formula and samples of some new metal alloy. Whatever it may be, it is probable that the Gestapo department, into whose holy of holies the visitor has been taken, already has full details in its possession. Even so, the visitor will not be told of this, although more may be already known than he would ever be able to discover and offer for sale. The matter on which he has been brought there will be discussed exhaustively, in his own language, no matter what that may be. He will be promised a reward commensurate with the value of his information before he leaves, but will not be told the amount: that will depend on how useful the man himself might prove. If the series of questions put to him elicits the fact that he could be used for some future purpose, he will be treated in very friendly fashion, and might even be invited to stay in Cologne for a day or two. Any hesitation or fears he might display over accepting the invitation would be removed.

The young man who, so far, had been no more than a businesslike, rather uninterested and even unfriendly sort of guide, would prove such an entertaining type of companion that his hitherto rather unattractive characteristics would be completely effaced, and he would so far devote himself to the visitor's comfort and amusement that it would not strike the visitor as strange if he were not left alone at any time. Meanwhile the guide would be engaged in sizing him up, minutely and accurately assessing character and capacities, so that any task entrusted to this new recruit would not be beyond his abilities. And, when the poor fool arrived back in his own country, he would never again be free.

In the room at headquarters in which he had been interviewed, no matter which one in the building it might be, he would find one setting and one pair of personalities only—they are all the same. The room—any one of these rooms—is not large: it is distempered in pale grey, bare and cold-looking. In the middle of the thinly-carpeted floor is a large, flat-topped desk, at which sits an absorbed and serious official, probably in the thirties or at most the early forties. His seriousness would be taken for granted, but not the reason for his absorption in his tasks, for neither on the desk nor anywhere else in the room would any papers be visible, nor books nor files—not even a scrap of paper, apart from the one on which this chief of a department might be writing, or which he might be studying. Each room contains one other chair in addition to that in use by the chief, and one other occupant—a youngish man, of the same type as the guide for the visitor, dressed either in well-fitting civilian clothes or, more probably, in the Nazi Party uniform. A hefty young fellow, always, one able to cope, physically, with almost any emergency. Unlike the older man at the desk, this youngster would appear neither serious nor absorbed, but, probably smoking a

cigarette, might be leaning on a corner of the desk,
looking as if there were nothing in the world worth
doing, and even if there were he would not be doing
it. He would certainly appear to take no interest at
all in the visitor's errand, and might even break in on
the interview with a flippant interjection—or at
least as nearly flippant as the German mentality is
capable of achieving, and the language of expressing.

But, if the visitor were self-possessed enough to
detach his mind from the official's questioning, and
from what might happen when he got back home,
long enough to give the lounging youngster a close
inspection, he would see a pair of eyes as hard as
flints, and lines about the square jaw that might
induce thoughts about concentration camps and
similar things. The man at the desk is the head of
his department of the Gestapo, whatever that
department may be: the younger man is his aide and
liaison with the outside world, completely trusted,
on terms of equality with his chief, and destined to
occupy the chair at the desk, when his turn comes.
He is, in fact, finishing his training and fitting himself to assume the responsibility of the department.

The entire filing system and records of every
room of this kind in the building are concentrated
on the ground floor, which is complete with every
mechnical and electrical device for the simplifica-
tion of clerical work. It is in charge of a number of
trusted men selected from the ranks of the Nazi
Party, and training for higher posts in the Gestapo
as they do their work. The entrance hall, which at
a first glance appears to be devoid of doors, will on
close inspection be seen to have sliding steel doors
on each side, so closely fitting and flush with the
walls as to be barely noticeable. Beyond them are
the record rooms.

Behind the staircase and thus not easy to find is a quite inconspicuous wooden door which opens on to a flight of stone steps, white and uncarpeted. At basement level is a metal, sound-proofed door, giving access to a corridor, and, on opening this door, a contrast presents itself: the broad corridor is thickly carpeted, and against its panelled walls stand pieces of exquisitely fine furniture—a small refectory table, an elaborately inlaid and lacquered Japanese chest, a lapis lazuli-framed Chinese screen, its black silken panels heavily embroidered with golden dragons and huge, lily-like flowers of the deepest blue. This screen stands before the door at one end of the corridor, and behind it (in the Cologne headquarters building, this) is the private office of Herr Wolfram Hacker, chief of the Western Division of the Gestapo. As one approaches the screen, there is on the left a very large reception room, furnished with all the luxury of an ornate modern drawing-room, and, facing it, an attendants' room.

Hacker could pass, at sight, as an English army colonel, as, no doubt, he sometimes does. His command of English is accentless, and in fact is that of a public school and 'varsity Englishman. He has a secretary, a girl of twenty-three or twenty-four, extremely well dressed and turned out, and in appearance so unaffectedly American that it causes no surprise when she speaks English with an American accent, using American idioms. Always with these two, in the event of any visitor materializing, is the inevitable lounging youth, who answers quite cheerfully and very politely to the name of Fritz. He has been known to express his regrets that his parents bestowed so unromantic a name on him, but consoles himself with the reflection that it is solidly German and undeniably Aryan.

A busy man, Herr Hacker. In fact, an exceedingly busy man. He is frequently absent from the grim house of secrets in the Salier Ring, and from Cologne. His secretary is occasionally absent at the same time, and Fritz invariably vanishes with his chief. His absences vary between visits to Berlin for conferences with Himmler, and trips to Amsterdam —it is nearly always Amsterdam, though he has occasionally gone to Brussels—to meet some nameless stranger or other. He never ventures farther out from Germany than these two cities. He speaks Dutch like a Hollander, and probably, on arrival in Holland also looks like a Hollander rather than an English colonel. He is fond of frankfurters with ham and sauerkraut, the German dish which the Dutch have so enthusiastically adopted and made their own, and he smokes Dutch "High Life" cigars, German gold-tipped cigarettes, Abdullas and Chesterfields with equal appreciation of the quality of each form of weed.

Whatever national type or character he may be representing, his characterization of it is perfect, and that without artificial aids of any kind. He has a way of changing from one to another very suddenly, and quite without warning, while, since he changes the language at the same time to fit the new character, the result is at times rather disconcerting. The precise English colonel becomes, in front of one's eyes, a slightly pompous but genially bourgeois Dutch burgomeister with a Leyden accent, or a fussily important French business man with a Provençal drawl or the harsh and heavy accents of the head of a Rouen house.

This chief of the Gestapo Western Division is a

very important personage. He takes orders only from Himmler, and at this building in the Salier Ring which he controls are gathered and sorted all the converging and intertwining threads of Gestapo work in the West, to be transmitted to that other building in Berlin, where sits Heinrich Himmler, Chief of the Gestapo.

A visitor to the Eastern Division headquarters in the Pragerstrasse at Dresden would find it virtually a replica of the Cologne building, and in Magdeburg there is little difference from the state of things in Cologne and Dresden, except that the atmosphere is a little more Prussian, a shade more military. Also, there are at Magdeburg a good many soldiers of the Reichswehr, in their field-grey uniforms, lounging about, and a very smart one with a fixed bayonet standing in each corridor. Why he is there is not quite clear to the casual visitor: he salutes everyone who passes him, very smartly and with unfailing conscientiousness—that is, if it is always the same soldier, which is open to doubt.

．　　　．　　　．　　　．　　　．

Thus the Gestapo, as put to external and internal uses—or misuses: what it does, what it is, and some sketch of the structure of its organization. It is, however, impossible to think of this secret and sinister body without question as to what manner of man controls it, and also as to the characters and natures of those other men in the Nazi hierarchy who use it for furtherance of their aims.

Heinrich Himmler was a school-teacher in pre-Nazi days, and at present appears to be forty-five to forty-eight years of age. He has made a success of his job, and in so doing has reached a position that satisfies his ambitions. He has used his position and powers for many different purposes since the day in 1932 when Goebbels raised him to his place. Among other things, he has used it to consolidate the position of Goering and undermine that of Goebbels, to destroy Captain Roehm and hundreds of others, and to discredit von Fritsch if not to murder him—to mention only a few things.

Himmler is a strong man with a cold and analytical mind, methodical and exact in its workings. In appearance he is dark, with expressionless face and eyes, a cynical half-smile—the type that merits the word "sardonic." He takes no action over anything until he has examined and decided on his course to the last particular; his passion for evidence and, where possible, proof, the ultimate *quod erat demonstrandum* of everything, is as great as that of Goebbels—greater, perhaps. He has failed only once in any move he has made: this was when, in 1938, he brought charges against General von Fritsch at Goering's instigation. That he failed then was not so much through his own fault as by reason of Hitler's bias. Probably, in revulsion from Goering's attempted incitement, Hitler remembered Roehm and the villa outside Munich that reeked of blood one June night: Roehm, the friend he himself had murdered.

In his judgments, Himmler is very impartial, and his decisions are always the results of fully objective reasoning. For his own purposes, he began as a creature of Goebbels. He transferred his allegiance to Goering when those purposes had been accomplished, and since then he has remained fairly constant to the interests of the man whom he helped so largely to become master of Germany. As Head of the Secret Police, Himmler is the right man in the right place: the credit of recognizing his

qualities—if there be any credit attaching to it—
belongs to Josef Goebbels, Reichsminister for
Propaganda.

For Goebbels there is but one justification, or
excuse: he knows his job, and does it. He is a
graduate of Berlin, a Doctor of Words—that is not
the exact translation of the wording in his diploma,
but it is the meaning, and it is Goebbels. He joined
the National Socialist Party in the earliest Munich
days, and followed the shabby, untidy man in the
shiny, threadbare blue serge suit, which was Adolf
Hitler. Followed him as if he were such a star as
that which guided the Magi, but with the hope of
receiving gifts, not bearing them with him. This
was not his first excursion into politics: he had
dabbled in Social Democracy and flirted with Communism, but, evidently, had given them up as
holding out no hopes for the future—his own
future. He made himself very useful to the struggg-
ling new party and adhered to it during the years of
its obscurity and its "persecution." Because of his
flair for publicity and his success in raising money
for the party funds, he made himself indispensable,
and rose as Hitler rose, in a position parallel with
that of Goering, but in a different field of action.

He is not only a Doctor of Words, but a Master
of Intrigue. His mind is twisted and mean: he is
incapable of taking a straight road to any given point
—he would prefer to make a sunken road for himself, and approach the objective from the rear. In
appearance he is dark and almost Semitic: his head
has odd and unexpected angles, and the skin of his
face gives an impression of being so tightly drawn as
to cause him pain. He is short, very slightly built,
and his club foot gives him a painful and halting
way of walking. Quite surprisingly his eyes are not

shifty, but straight-gazing—boring, almost—and glittering with the abundance of malice there is in the man. He has perfect and gleamingly white teeth.

His position may or may not be secure: Goering tolerates him for one reason and one only—the Doctor of Words is worthy of his hire; Goering takes care that he earns it all the time.

.　　.　　.　　.　　.

Field-Marshal Hermann Goering is Chief of the Air Force of the Reich not only because he was a member of von Richthofen's air squadron in the last war, but also because the military *bloc* would not let him enter the army as long as they had the power to keep him out—not even when he promoted himself in one step from a junior captaincy to the rank of General. He took command of the Air Force because he could wait no longer for a commanding position in something or other of a military nature, and, after all, being Prime Minister of Prussia with no separate Prussia to give reality to the title was not very satisfying. Thus he made himself head of the Air Force even though it did not exist at the time, and probably consoled himself with the reflection that, at least, he could design a uniform to suit himself.

His vanity and impatience are not indications of weakness. He is obstinate and extravagantly ambitious, but his quality of brutal, ruthless directness makes his advancement irresistible. This directness of purpose, or rather of action, is ponderous in its inevitability, crushing all opposition that is not paralysed before it can come to action. To consider the influence of such a character over such an emotional type as is represented by Hitler is to realize the main cause of Goering's ascendancy: beginning as a follower, he rose to mastery.

There is obviously no room for intrigue in such a personality as his: that deficiency in his make-up is supplied by Himmler. He has no tricks, uses no subterfuges: if he wants anything, he simply takes it, as does the big bully at school. Like the bully, he gets away with whatever it may be, nobody attempting to stop him.

Hitler trusts and is influenced by him to an extraordinary extent. It gave the Fuehrer as much childish pleasure to hand to the Field-Marshal a baton studded with jewels as big as walnuts, as the receipt of the costly toy gave Goering—and as it gives him to carry the thing about. His appearance is too well-known from photographs and news-reels to need any description.

Baron Franz von Papen, ambassador-extraordinary in the most literal sense of the words. Meet the Baron.

He has combined diplomacy with politics, and intrigue with both, for so long that he is now unable to distinguish one from the other, or to use the technique of any of them separately. As a diplomatic representative of Germany before the last war, he interfered in the politics of his own country equally with those of the country to which he was accredited, and in addition gratuitously assumed control of espionage. In post-war Germany he intrigued both with and against every political party in turn. He obtained the protection of von Hindenburg by means of his friendship with the aged Marshal, only to intrigue against him as President, and finally used him to secure the uneasy Chancellorship of the Reich, which he eventually relinquished to Hitler. His knowledge of the finesse of diplomacy is scanty, and his abilities are more suited to plain sabotage—as in the United States— and to the instigation to murder and incitement to assassination, as in Austria. Still, he throws him- self into the mazes of Nazi intrigue with a species of joyous and irresponsible *abandon* that has a shade of incredibility about it.

Both Hitler and the National Socialist Party owe a good deal to this passion of his for double-dealing: without von Papen's help, Hitler might have had to wait some while beyond 1933 for the place that the then Chancellor was willing to hand over to him. Intrigue means more to the man than position or power: it gives him an illusion of power which is far more satisfying to such a nature as his.

When Berlin offered no more opportunities for the use of his peculiar talents, he was quite content to go and begin activities in Austria, and when the curtain fell and the stage was darkened in Vienna, he packed his props and headed for Stamboul, cheerfully enough. The applause for his act on the Turkish stage has yet to begin, and he will need all his bag of tricks to secure an encore.

In some ways not unlike this von Papen is Herr Joachim von Ribbentrop, member of Hitler's Secret Council of Four, German Foreign Minister and intimate adviser on foreign affairs to the leaders of the Nazi Party—the other leaders, that is. He is victim of a phobia, an intense aversion to the English people, English customs, the English men- tality, and everything else that is English—England itself, even. This Anglophobia is so virulent, so persistent, as to be an integral part of the man. He deliberately assumed the duties of German Ambassador in England while virtually Foreign Minister of the Reich, in order to make certain that nobody less antagonistic than himself should hold the post, or advise the German Government as to English intentions and the trend of English politics. A reason for his fundamental dislike of all things English can be found in the inflexibility of the Prussian mind, of which von Ribbentrop is fully typical: the type is without exception infuriated on recognizing the quality which it can only describe as the "superiority" of the English: it is a common condition, and may be found even in non-Prussian Germans; the only possible cure for it is a sense of humour, and no way of grafting any such thing on to the German character has yet been discovered.

So long as von Ribbentrop has any hand in the direction of German foreign policy, just so long will he direct it away from England by every means at his command. His personality is not impressive, his appearance greyly insignificant. He owes his rise in the Nazi Party to his wealth, or rather to that of his wife. She is the daughter of the great wine merchant for whom he worked, and, up to 1932, his Berlin house was the secret rendezvous of von Papen and the Nazi leaders: it was there that many of von Papen's sinister plots were elaborated. Von Ribbentrop's initial reward for giving house-room to the Party leaders was a minor government post as Minister for Disarmament, whatever that may have meant, in the Hitler régime of 1934. He has continued to rise.

.   .   .   .   .

Adolf Hitler.

The man responsible—nominally, at least—for everything.

The less that one knows about this extraordinary man, the easier it is to write about him—as the daily press makes evident. The more one knows of him, the more difficult becomes description, possibly because Adolf Hitler does not even know himself.

In appearance he is not impressive; already he is inclined to the usual Teutonic shapelessness that comes with middle age. He has few of the characteristics which Germans associate with their "Aryanism." Straight lips and nose and eyebrows, straight lines of jaw and forehead and neck, are not his. The clothes he wears are neither good nor well cut; he is entirely devoid of personal vanity. His habits were always ascetic, and are becoming more so. For years he has neither smoked nor taken alcohol, and often he has eaten one meal a day, that consisting of a little spinach and a fried egg. He is emotional and easily moved to tears under certain conditions—unkind or stupid critics might term him neurotic.

With all this he has a personality at once magnetic and compelling: it is expressed by means of his eyes —eyes that have the power to conjure up visions with which he not only surrounds himself, but envelops whatever audience he may be facing— dreams and hopes that he transforms to tangible, living realities—for the time. That is the secret of his hold over German youth and German women. They flock to him as pilgrims of old crowded to meet the preacher credited with the power to heal.

Adolf Hitler is not one man, nor two: he is legion. The differing facets which exist in an ordinary character are, in him, entirely different personalities. No matter which he may be using, it is expressed and made dominant by the compelling urgency of those eyes of his. His attitude toward life is undoubtedly due to the repressions of his early years—thwarted ambitions, the injustice of the Austrians who deprived him of his citizenship and of his "heimat." This attitude of his is expressed in one unvarying determination—to regenerate the youth of Germany, and through them the whole of humanity, with himself as the ideal, the leader who will point the way. There is room in his mind for only this purpose, which he has pursued with a singleness of aim that has become fanatical, megalomaniac.

In 1933 he became Chancellor of the Reich, and a little later President. In his own mind he became neither, but the Reichsfuehrer—Leader of the German People. That he has remained, becoming ever more exalted—exalté is a more fitting word for it—and mystic as he sees the world reborn, following after him. He is lost in the white light that began as idealism, and has gone on to megalomania.

Chancellor and President he is in name, but to himself he is world-leader, which makes clear the ease with which Goering and the clique that is Prussianism have used both him and the German State to their own ends, and how simple they have found it to interpret his dreams into world domination. Stripped of his magnetism, Hitler is curiously defenceless, fumbling and hesitant and a little pitiable; and his magnetism is only effective when he uses it as Reichsfuehrer, not as President or Chancellor. In his sincerity—for the man is sincere—he has let his dreams absorb and eventually betray him, and the white light in which he sees his visions has turned to crimson.

It is possible to pity Adolf Hitler.